Basic Personal Finance

*A Practical Guide to Financial
Wellbeing*

Len Cabrera, PhD
Richard Fullerton, PhD

ISBN 978-0-9988609-0-9
ISBN 978-0-9988609-1-6 (ebook)

Dedicated to Brig Gen Richard A. Fullerton, USAF (ret), 10 Aug 1961 – 12 Dec 2016. The smartest man I ever worked for, yet humble, caring, and always willing to listen to others. He kept me grounded and (despite my best efforts) helped minimize bureaucratic squabbles. He was my boss, mentor, role-model, colleague, and friend. He will be missed.

– Len Cabrera, March 2017

Contents

Preface (and Disclaimer)

This book is based on the classroom handout, "Introduction to Financial Planning and Investing for Cadets," written by Richard Fullerton in October 2007, in which he wrote: "I hope this is just the beginning of a lifetime of learning about financial planning and investing for you. There are more than just monetary rewards to be gained from a lifetime of learning." We expanded the original to include more general advice on "adulting" and to be more applicable to those not going into the military. Most of the expansion is based on interactions with students outside of the classroom, like discovering they didn't know how to write a check. Our goal was to achieve a balance between academic research, classroom textbook, and practical advice to help young adults start a successful path to financial wellbeing.

Chapter 1 starts with a very brief explanation of economics, and introduces the ten rules of thumb from the original work. Following these rules is not guaranteed to make the reader wealthy and successful, but it will greatly increase the chances of avoiding financial pitfalls that ensnare many people. The remainder of the book attempts to present material in a logical order: compensation and taxes, budgeting, banking, retirement, investment, and insurance. The final chapter was added to help with big decisions: home and automobile purchases. We also added an appendix on financial math for those who want to roll back the algebraic curtain and see where the numbers come from.

Overall, the book is only a beginner's guide to personal finance that includes very basic advice on financial planning and investing. It highlights some common investment mistakes and makes general advice based on historic market data and the personal experience of the authors, neither of whom is a Certified Financial Advisor. It does not offer "get-rich-quick" schemes, but encourages the safest, proven way to accumulate wealth via disciplined saving and patient, long-term investing. As always, past performance in the marketplace is never a guarantee of future success.

Because of the vagaries of ebook translators, we will make tables, images, and formulas available at www.lencabrera.com. The site will also contain support material for those who want to use the book for teaching.

About the Authors

Len Cabrera has a PhD in economics from the University of Florida, an MS in operations research from Stanford University, and an MBA from the University of West Florida. He taught at the United States Air Force Academy for seven years, specializing in microeconomic theory and optimization theory.

Richard Fullerton earned his PhD in economics from the University of Texas at Austin. He taught at the United States Air Force Academy for sixteen years, serving as Permanent Professor and Department Head of Economics and Geosciences from 2001 to 2014.

Chapter 1. Introduction

1.1. Economics and Scarcity

Scarcity is a fact of life, and it's the first and most basic lesson in the study of economics. Whether it's cars, homes, entertainment, education, medicine, food, healthcare, clothes, or any other "good," people always want more than they have or can afford. More importantly, *you* will always want more than you can afford, as well. You will have to make tough financial choices in life. So, if you must make some hard decisions, it's better to have a plan now to make the most of what you've got, rather than blindly stumbling through and hoping for the best.

This book should help you make better decisions by learning from our experience. It's always better to learn from the mistakes of others than from your own. While you should obviously read the entire book, here are rules of thumb that summarize what you should learn.

1.2. Ten Rules of Thumb

Search the internet and you will find hundreds of websites offering rules of thumb for financial success. Here are ten favorites to help you be successful with your finances:

1. Pay yourself first! Start now, and save at least 10% of your monthly pre-tax income.

Scarcity does not disappear when you earn more income. Do not fool yourself into thinking it will be easier to save later. The time to start saving is today. Sure, you don't make as much money now as you will in the future, but you don't have as many expenses or obligations either. **Compound interest** is an incredibly powerful force, so the earlier you begin to save, the more time you'll have for compounding.

The easiest way to save is to make it a habit and pay yourself as soon as you get your paycheck. Don't wait until the end of the month to save whatever money is left over—there won't be any. There are many articles and studies that show living expenses tend to increase with income, and the amount of money people think they need to retire comfortably is always higher than the amount they have saved, even for millionaires.

Pay yourself first by setting up an automatic payroll deduction from your paycheck so the money is taken out before you have an opportunity to spend it. You may be able to do this through your employer's payroll program, or you can set up an automatic withdrawal through your bank. With an automatic deduction, you'll be surprised how little you'll miss the money. And if you take care of your savings first, you can spend the rest guilt free. We recommend saving at least 10% of each paycheck to start. Then, increase your savings percentage with each pay raise.

2. Develop a budget.

Everyone needs a budget. The bestselling book, *The Millionaire Next Door*, reveals that the majority of wealthy people in America "became millionaires by budgeting and controlling expenses."[1] Without having a budget, it is difficult to know what you can afford and what you cannot. A budget also helps you be disciplined with your spending and enables you to follow rule number one: pay yourself first!

If the typical millionaire keeps a budget, shouldn't you, too? A big reason they became millionaires is because they had a budget. The authors of *The Millionaire Next Door* call it "playing great defense" with your finances.[2]

3. Keep your debt payments under control.

Many experts suggest that your total house payment should be no more than 28% of your monthly income, and your total monthly debt payments (which include your mortgage, car loans, credit card payments, etc.) should be less than 36% of your gross monthly income.[3] If your monthly debt payments exceed these amounts, you should probably cut back on your spending until you get your debt under control.

---

[1] Stanley and Danko, p40
[2] Stanley and Danko, p36
[3] "How Much House Can I Afford." Bankrate.com

4. Understand the difference between "good debt" and "bad debt."

Bad debts are purchases that begin depreciating (dropping in value) as soon as you purchase the items, such as clothes, video games, computers, and stereos. Good debts are for items that can create value, such as student loans for education or a home mortgage that has the potential to appreciate in value. *Do all you can to avoid bad debt.* If you are incurring a lot of bad debt, you are living beyond your means and sacrificing your future financial wellbeing.

5. Insure yourself against catastrophic loss, but don't over insure.

You need enough insurance to avoid being financially wiped out by an accident or act of nature. Liability insurance is a must in our litigious society. On the other hand, in the long run you will usually save money by maintaining higher deductibles on your auto and home insurance, and avoiding specialty insurance products like extended warranties and traveler's insurance.

6. Maintain an emergency expense fund.

Life is full of unexpected events; some are good and some are bad. You may need money quickly for good or bad events–to pay off unexpected debts if you are in an accident or, perhaps, to take advantage of unexpected investment opportunities should they arise. An emergency account is probably sufficient if it's worth one or two months of your pay and is reasonably accessible. (But be sure to keep this money in an account that earns interest–you need to be able to access the money, but there's no need to forego earning a return on it, as well.)

An example of the need for an emergency expense fund comes from a co-worker who transferred from an Army post to the Air Force Academy. In the bureaucratic shuffle between services, his paychecks were forgotten for three pay periods. Fortunately, he had enough money set aside to cover his expenses until DFAS could straighten it out and pay him what he was owed.

7. Diversify your portfolio.

Don't put all of your investment eggs in one basket. If you invest in the stock market, consider starting with a no-load index fund or a broadly diversified no-load mutual fund. Diversifying your portfolio will help prevent you from being wiped out by an unforeseen bankruptcy by one company (e.g., Enron) or a drop in one sector of the economy.

8. Don't ignore opportunity costs.

Opportunity cost is the most valuable thing you give up by your investment choice. If you have $5,000 stashed away in a savings account earning 1% interest, but are also making the minimum payment against a $2,000 credit card bill that charges you 16% interest, then you are not paying attention to the opportunity cost of having your money in the savings account. If you count the opportunity cost, you are really giving up 15% in foregone earnings on $2,000 of your savings account–because that is the difference between what you are earning on the account and what you are paying on your credit card bill. Pay off your credit card bill and stop carrying a balance because those interest charges are going to sink you.

9. Negotiating is good; competition is great.

When making a purchase or investment, look around and examine your alternatives. Sales persons will try to convince you to make an immediate decision, often saying their offer is good for a limited time only. Rarely is that actually the case. *Competition* makes markets efficient. If you overlook the competition and try to rely only on your own negotiating skills, more often than not you will be disappointed. The sales person almost always has more information and more experience than you–so market competition is often your best bet for making a good deal.

10. Don't count on being bailed out in retirement by Social Security.

The demographics are working against your generation, and it is unlikely Social Security will be your primary income source if you want a comfortable standard of living in retirement. This means it is up to you to ensure your retirement savings will provide adequate income during your golden years. How big of a nest egg should you have? The bestselling book, *The Millionaire Next Door*, has a simple formula for computing what a strong net worth looks like for individuals today:[4]

$$\text{age} \times \text{pretax income} \div 10$$

If you are 30 years old earning $70,000 a year, you should have a net worth of $210,000 or more. If you are 40 making $120,000 per year, you should have a net worth of $480,000. If you want to be numbered among America's "wealthy," double these amounts.

Easy enough, right? Ten simple rules that will improve your chances of financial success. Of course, there are non-financial rules that have an even bigger impact on whether you live a successful life (e.g., don't do drugs, don't get arrested, etc.). Violating those rules will not necessarily ruin your life, but they will definitely make things harder. This book only focuses on the financial side.

Assuming you don't already have a large fortune, following the first step (pay yourself first!) means you need to get paid. The next chapter discusses compensation.

---

[4] Stanley and Danko, p13

Chapter 2. Compensation & Taxes

2.1. Salary vs. Wage

If you are like most people, chances are the only resource you have available to you early in life is your own labor. Unless you want to be self-sufficient and live a subsistence lifestyle (growing your own food, making your own clothes, building your own house, etc.), you must interact in markets to obtain the goods and services you want. You're probably already well familiar with participating in a market as a buyer, but eventually you will need to participate as a seller. You have to convert your one resource (labor) into money. That's not fun, so it's called work.

Compensation for work can be monetary or non-monetary (next section). Monetary compensation can be a fixed amount (**salary**) or an hourly amount (**wage**). Typically a salary is paid for "white collar" (i.e., office-type) work, and hourly wages are paid for "blue collar" (manual) work, but there are no specific rules on certain types of work paying one way or the other. For example, "lawyering" is considered white collar work, but they typically bill by the hour, while many trades, like plumbers and electricians, charge by the job, not by the hour. A salaried employee will typically be paid once or twice a month, and their work is expected to be done regardless of hours (within reason). An hourly employee usually has to punch in and out of a time clock to track the hours worked. These employees are typically paid every week or every two weeks, and get overtime pay if they exceed certain limits (usually 8 hours a day or 40 hours a week).

As in every other market, there are two ways to sell your product: lower price or better quality. In this case, lower price means accepting a lower salary or wage than your competition (i.e., other potential workers). Most people do not want to do this because they want to receive as high a salary or wage as possible. (Similarly, most retailers would prefer you pay full price (or more!) when buying their wares.) In a slow economy, however, there will always be people willing to do your job for less money... and your boss knows it. The more likely way to get (and keep) a job is to provide a quality product. You can do this by investing in yourself through education or job training. You also do this by providing exactly what your customer (boss) wants and then some.

This is admittedly anecdotal, but in our experience talking to many business owners over the last fifteen years, when asked what the hardest part of business ownership is, they all said the same thing: finding good employees. If you show up on time and always provide your best effort, your employer will recognize and appreciate you. In larger companies (and the military), however, your hard work may not be immediately recognized because there are fixed rules for compensation and pay raises. Military compensation is discussed in Appendix A.

While you have some influence on your pay, realize the labor market works like any other market: it is governed by supply and demand. If you choose a profession that many other people also choose, the supply will be higher, and compensation will be lower. Similarly, if you choose a skill that has no demand in the labor market, you will not make much money. This frequently happens when trying to turn a "passion" into a career. If you're not getting paid for it, it's a hobby. If you can monetize your passion, consider yourself one of the lucky few.

2.2. Non-Monetary Compensation (i.e., Benefits)

Non-monetary compensation is sometimes called "fringe benefits" or simply benefits. It includes anything an employer provides other than salary or wages. While the practice is not new or unique to the United States, the term dates back to World War II, when firms used benefits to attract workers because the War Labor Board prohibited wage increases.

Examples of benefits include:

- Paid time off
- Insurance programs (health, vision, dental, and/or life insurance)

- Retirement programs (tax-deferred savings options, often with matching contributions)
- Flex-time (adjusting work start and end times rather than a fixed 9-5 job)
- Tuition assistance
- Free or discounted parking
- Gym memberships
- Childcare
- Company car
- Free food

The types of benefits a company provides are based on several factors, including the competitiveness of the labor market in that industry, the company's management philosophy, and the tax rules that apply to the benefits. There are also legal requirements for certain benefits that must be provided. For example, the Affordable Care Act requires employers with 50 or more full-time (i.e., 30+ hours) workers to provide health insurance or pay a fine.[5]

Typically, entry-level employees do not have much bargaining power when it comes to benefits and accept whatever standard benefits package is offered. As the labor market tightens (i.e., fewer workers available to hire) or a worker's skills become more unique and sought after, the ability to request (even demand) certain benefits increases. For example, companies trying to hire a specific person for a job are likely to offer whatever the person requests. This is commonly seen when hiring a new Chief Executive Officer, a college football coach, or a celebrity performer.

2.3. Tax Basics

Sadly, when you get compensated for work, you have to pay taxes just like every other citizen. Unless you are self-employed or a contract (1099[6]) worker, you will notice that taxes are subtracted each month from your paycheck to cover:

---

[5] USSBA, "Employers with 50 or More Employees"
[6] IRS Form 1099 is used to report income to non-employees. A 1099-MISC must be issued to contractors by clients who pay them over $600 a year. There

- Federal income tax
- Federal Insurance Contributions Act (FICA) taxes for Social Security and Medicare
- State income tax

Collectively, these taxes can take a sizable bite out of your paycheck.

Federal Income Tax. Each year, Americans must file their federal income tax returns with the Internal Revenue Service (IRS) by April 15th or obtain an extension of their filing date to avoid being penalized by the IRS. A tax return basically adds up your income from all sources (to compute **adjusted gross income** or AGI) and makes adjustments based on the tax laws to compute your **taxable income**. **Exemptions** are a standard amount of money you subtract from AGI based on the number of dependents you claim.[7] **Deductions** are amounts you can subtract from AGI for engaging in specific activities (charitable donations, tuition expenses, healthcare costs, property taxes, etc.). Unless you pay mortgage interest or are exceptionally charitable, you'll likely take a standard deduction early in your life, which greatly simplifies your tax preparation and likely results in a lower taxable income.[8] The amount of tax you owe is based on your taxable income. This amount is compared to the income tax you paid during the year (via paycheck withholding). If the difference is positive, you must pay the difference (via Form 1040-V). If you overpaid your taxes, you will receive a **refund**.

For younger workers, federal income tax computation is fairly straightforward. You may be able to complete and file your federal income tax forms yourself just using the instructions provided with the tax form–which will be either an IRS Form 1040EZ, 1040A, or 1040, depending on the complexity of your tax situation (how many dependents you have, how many deductions you have, the types of income you have, etc.). Later, as the complexity of your taxes grows, along with your

---

are other types of 1099s (-B, -C, -DIV, -INT, -R), which you can read about at irs.gov.

[7] For 2017, the standard exemption was $4,050 per dependent (1040 p2)

[8] For 2017, the standard deduction for a single filer with no dependents was $6,300 (1040 p2)

number of dependents and streams of earnings and income, you may find it helpful to purchase tax computation software such as TurboTax, H&R Block, TaxAct, or TaxSlayer. If your financial situation is complex, you may also need to consult a tax professional for assistance in completing your return.

How much federal income tax can you expect to pay each year? To understand your tax liability, it is important to know that the U.S. federal government has a **progressive rate** income tax system. A progressive rate system means there are increasing marginal rates (i.e., the amount you pay for additional dollars of income). Our progressive rate system is also a **progressive tax**, meaning that people with larger incomes pay an increasingly higher percentage of their income in taxes–under the assumption that they have more of an ability to pay than people with lower incomes. (While this book is not intended to discuss tax policy, note that a single rate tax system with a common deduction is also a progressive tax. A progressive rate tax is like a progressive tax on steroids.) The table below shows the incremental federal income tax rates for a single filer in tax year 2016.[9]

U.S. Tax Brackets 2016	
Taxable Income	Marginal Rate
$0 – $9,275	10%
$9275 – $37,650	15%
$37,650 – $91,150	25%
$91,150 – $190,150	28%
$190,150 – $413,350	33%
$413,350 – $415,050	35%
$415, 050 and up	39.6%

What does this mean? Let's do a quick calculation of federal income tax for the "typical" Second Lieutenant (see Appendix A on military compensation and Appendix B for completed sample tax forms). At the start of the year, she will receive a W-2 Wage and Tax Statement from her employer. This form will

---

[9] 1040 Instructions p103

show her "wages, salaries, and other compensation" subject to taxes for the previous year (box 1). The form will also show how much tax was withheld over the course of the year (box 2). For our fictitious example, let's suppose our 2Lt's W-2 shows $36,417.60 in box 1 and a tax withholding of $3641. We'll also assume the 2Lt got a good start on savings and investments and earned an additional $500 in 2016 on her investments (which would be reported on a Form 1099-DIV or 1099-INT). Since her income and tax situation are so simple, we will use the IRS form 1040EZ when filing her income tax. The 2Lt's income in 2016 subject to federal taxes was:

Air Force Pay (Line 1)	$36,417
Investment Interest (Line 2)	$500
Total, AGI (Line 4)	$36,917

Note that we dropped the cents when filling out the form for simplicity. For 2016, our single 2Lt can claim herself as an exemption ($4,050), and she can claim the standard deduction ($6,300) on her federal taxes. Therefore, on line 5 of the 1040EZ, her adjusted gross income is reduced by $10,350. This means her total taxable income (Line 6) for 2016 was $36,917 − $10,350 = $26,567

With a total taxable income of $26,567, how much federal income tax does she owe for 2016? From the tax table, we can look up that she owed $3,523 in federal income tax (Line 10 of 1040EZ). The table uses $50 increments of taxable income so it's not the same as if we use the tax brackets to directly compute the tax owed: 10% of her first $9,275 of income ($927), plus 15% on the remainder ($0.15(26,657 − 9275) = $2,594$) equals a total tax of $927 + $2,594 = $3,521$.

Newer tax forms have a line to potentially increase the taxes owed if the filer did not fulfill their "individual responsibility" by having healthcare coverage that satisfies the requirements of the Affordable Care Act (as evidenced by a Form 1095-B provided by the employer or insurance provider). In this case, our 2Lt had full-year coverage from the military healthcare system, so the tax owed remains at $3,523 on line 12.

Her withholding exceeds the amount owed. Therefore, our 2Lt is due a refund of $3,641 − $3,523 = $118. If this amount were very large, our 2Lt could reduce her withholding in the following year by updating her IRS Form W-4 Employee's Withholding Allowance Certificate with her employer. The W-4 changes withholding by allowing you to declare your filing status, set the number of "allowances," and declare a specific additional amount to withhold. Be careful when doing this because you may owe a penalty if you do not withhold at least 90% of what you owe.[10]

If our 2Lt wanted to completely break even and neither pay money nor receive a refund, she would set a specific withholding amount equal to $3,523/12 = $293.58. Note, however, that this amount is based on 2016 income, not 2017, so doing so is not guaranteed to balance out the tax owed in 2017 (but we'll use this figure in the next chapter for a budget example).

FICA Taxes. The Federal Insurance Contributions Act (FICA), passed in the 1930s, imposed an employment tax to fund Old-Age, Survivors, and Disability Insurance (OASDI), also called Social Security. In the 1960s, the FICA tax added payments to Medicare (i.e., single-payer health insurance for the elderly). The Social Security tax is 6.2% and the Medicare tax is 1.45%, each paid by both employees and employers. (The full 12.4% and 2.9% taxes are paid by people who are self-employed.)

Many people consider these to be **flat taxes** (the percentage withheld is a constant), but in reality, the Social Security tax is only collected on income up to a certain amount, so it is a flat tax up to that point, and then the tax collected as a percentage of income declines, making it a **regressive tax**. The income limit was fixed for the first 13 years of OASDI, but it has increased every year since 1972. The limit in 2017 was $127,200.[11]

The Medicare tax is fixed up to $200,000. All income beyond that amount is subject to an additional 0.9% tax for the

---

[10] irs.gov Topic 306
[11] USSSA, "Contribution and Benefit Bases, 1937-2017"

employee. There is no matching contribution from the employer above the $200,000 threshold.

So, for our 2Lt who earned $36,417.60, the military withheld 6.2% x $36,417.60 = $2,257.89 to cover Social Security taxes and 1.45% x $36,417.60 = $528.06 for Medicare, as reflected in the W-2 in Appendix B. If we assume our 2Lt earned the same income each month, the FICA portion of the 2Lt's pay statement would show monthly withholding of $188.16 and $44.01. We'll use these numbers in the next chapter when developing a budget.

State Income Tax. Finally, our 2Lt must also pay state income tax on her salary. State income tax rates vary dramatically across the U.S. For example, Colorado residents pay a flat income tax rate of 4.63%. New Jersey residents pay a progressive rate income tax which varies from 1.4% for lower wage earners to 8.97% for higher wage earners. Alaska, Florida, Nevada, South Dakota, Texas, Washington, and Wyoming currently have no state income tax.[12]

Our 2Lt is lucky because her W-2 shows Florida as her state of residence. Military members have the state they lived in when entering the military as their "home of record" for tax purposes. Once they get stationed in a state with better tax laws, they are allowed to change their official residence for tax purposes. Residency requirements vary from state to state, but generally involve getting a driver's license and voter registration in that state. Military members can keep their state residency after they leave the state, as long as they stay on active duty in the military.

Now that you know about compensation and taxes, it's time to learn how to manage that money by developing a plan for how to spend (and save) it. That's called a budget.

---

[12] "State Individual Income Tax Rates and Brackets for 2016." TaxFoundation.org

Chapter 3. Budgeting

The easiest way to get in trouble with money is to not pay attention to it. Sadly, those who make the least are most likely to get in trouble–just look at the number of paycheck loan stores in poorer neighborhoods. Making a budget is essential to your personal financial health, especially when your life situation changes (promotion, pay raise, marriage, moving, etc.). A budget provides discipline in your spending and enables you to accomplish rule number one: pay yourself first.

3.1. How to Budget

Making a budget is not difficult. It can be as simple as using a pen and paper, although tracking with a spreadsheet is easier. There are also many free online tools you can use to budget, but always be careful of what a website may be trying to sell you or what information they are trying to get from you. *U.S. News and World Report* recommends several free sites: mint.com, pearbudget.com, levelmoney.com, and gnucash.org.[13]

When budgeting, it is important to know how much money is coming in to ensure expenditures do not exceed that amount. Many people will argue that a budget is unnecessary because the expenses are what they are going to be, but once you start tracking your expenses, you'll quickly find out just how much of it is discretionary. For example, you don't *need* the 200-channel cable package or 400GB data plan for your smart phone. You might be shocked by how much frivolous spending you do (e.g., ATM fees) when you actually track where your money goes.

Start with your best estimate of after-tax income. Next, estimate your expenses as realistically as possible. There are some items that are not monthly expenses. In these cases, get as close to a monthly average as possible. For example, if you own a home and pay your own property taxes (versus having it paid through escrow; see Chapter 5), you will have a very large tax bill once or twice a year. Spread that cost over 12 months for the purposes of budgeting.

---

[13] Peterson

Here is a list of categories to consider for your budget:

- Saving - pay yourself first! (Chapters 7 & 8 discuss what to do with this money.)
- Housing - rent or mortgage, insurance, maintenance, repairs, taxes
- Utilities - gas, water, electric, trash, phone, cable, internet
- Food
- Transportation - bus and subway fares, car (payment, insurance, gas, maintenance), tolls, parking
- Personal care - haircuts, toiletries, clothes, laundry, dry cleaning
- Healthcare - insurance, copays, dentist, glasses, etc.
- Debt payments - student loans, credit cards, etc.
- Charity - it's easier to give when you plan to give
- Entertainment - dining out, movies, games, travel, etc.

Note that entertainment was listed last. This is usually the biggest source of nonessential items in a budget. Still, there are plenty of areas in the budget that can be cut if necessary, even if the savings may not be possible immediately. For example, if your rent payment is higher than you would like, you can lower it by moving or finding a roommate, neither of which is an immediate solution.

Once you create a budget, track your actual expenses to see how close you come to the budget you created. The point is not to become obsessive about money or saving every receipt. Creating the budget is a good mental exercise to help you see where you stand, but the tracking portion is the part that instills discipline in your financial affairs. When you enter frivolous purchases into whatever tool you use to track the budget, you get immediate feedback that you may not be doing the best you can with your finances.

3.2. Sample Budget

In the previous chapter, we looked at the income and taxes paid by a 2Lt. Now that we have determined how much she will earn, and how much she will pay in taxes, we can go about creating a monthly budget for her. Recall her monthly income and taxes:

Income:

Basic Pay	$3,034.80
BAS	$253.63
BAH (COS, no dependents)	$1,350.00
Monthly Pre-tax Pay and Allowances	$4,638.43

Taxes:

Federal Income Tax	$293.58
FICA Taxes	$232.17
State Income Tax (FL resident)	$0
Monthly Tax Withheld	$525.75

From these calculations we see our 2Lt has a monthly after-tax disposable income of $4,113. (Tracking cents in the budget plan is not necessary.) Now, let's examine her estimated expenses. The purpose here is to illustrate how to go about making a realistic budget using personal circumstances.

She was a conscientious student at the Air Force Academy and paid attention in her core economics course–so she knows it is imperative that she *pays herself first*. As a result, she already set up a monthly automatic savings/investment withdrawal from her paycheck of $500 (a little over 10% of her pre-tax income).

Another easy budget item is her automobile expense. She took out a low-interest car loan in her senior year. The loan was for $30,000, to be paid off over 5 years at 3% interest. The loan rate calculator at http://tcalc.timevalue.com tells us her monthly payment is $539.[14] She already knows her yearly auto insurance premium for liability, collision, and comprehensive is $1,200, so she budgets $100 per month for auto insurance.

Her other automobile expenses are not as exact. She has to estimate what she'll spend for gas and maintenance. Her car gets an average of 26 miles to the gallon (mostly in-town driving), and she expects to drive 12,000 miles per year. So, she

---

[14] Or she can compute it herself after reading Appendix E; Excel formula "=PMT(.03/12,60,-30000)"

estimates a need to purchase 462 gallons of gas this year. That is 38 gallons per month, on average. At $3 per gallon, that is $115 per month just for gasoline! She estimates she will need an average of $40 per month more to cover maintenance costs for her car. Thus, she plans on needing about $155 per month for her car expenses. (The national average for single-person households was $234 per month for gas, oil, and maintenance in 2014, so she may be optimistic with her estimate, but that could be OK since it is a newer car.[15])

She would like to rent a nice apartment within an easy commute to her job, which costs $1,200 per month. (Making this budget will let her know if she can afford to live there.) She knows it will cost more than just rent, but is not familiar with the cost of utilities in the area. She can pursue several alternatives: she can ask the apartment complex management for typical utility costs, she can contact the local utility company about typical costs, or she can do a little online research for general numbers. Since she's developing her budget after business hours, it's simplest to just search online, and she finds a newspaper article on local utility rates. She sees the average cost in Colorado Springs for electric, gas, and water adds up to $201.85 per month.[16] Fortunately, trash service is included in the apartment's rent. A final cost will be renter's insurance to protect her belongings, should anything happen to the apartment. She knows that will cost about $200 per year, so she budgets another $16 per month. Therefore, her anticipated housing expense per month is $1,418.

The only other "easy" expenses she can think of are her cell phone and cable/internet service. The phone is under contract for $60 per month, so that is fixed. The other expense has some flexibility depending on how much she wants to use. Unfortunately, her preferred apartment complex does not allow satellite dishes, so she is stuck with the local cable provider. She can check their website for different package prices and decides to compare other alternatives. She looks into other

---

[15] If you'd rather use consumer averages, a summary of the latest (2014) BLS Consumer Expenditure Report Table 5 is provided in Appendix C. You can find the most recent report at https://www.bls.gov/cex/csxreport.htm

[16] Larimer

internet providers and finds a plan for only $30 per month (an introductory price good for 12 months). She plans to use an online streaming service for another $20 a month. Combined, these two will save her about $30 per month on the cheapest cable/internet package she found.

She's unsure of other expenses, but she remembers learning about the U.S. Bureau of Labor Statistics Consumer Expenditure Survey and she looks up the latest version to see what other expenses she may need to consider. From the report she finds expenses for:

Item	Yearly	Monthly
Food at home	$2,101	$175
Food away from home	$1,536	$128
Household furnishings	$844	$70
Apparel & services	$802	$67
Healthcare	$2,517	$210
Personal care products & services	$400	$34
Life & other personal insurance	$136	$12

She's not sure how much she'll be eating at home or away, but she knows she's a picky eater so she decides to combine the food entries and pad the number to $350 each month for budget purposes. Since she's just starting up her household, she also thinks it would be prudent to plan to spend more than the average $70 per month on furnishings. She picks $105 per month, which is 50% more than the average in the BLS report.

For apparel and personal care products, she decides to go with the average values for her budget... one perk to wearing a uniform every day. She makes a note to keep track to see how much she actually spends on these items. The other two items are things she hadn't considered. Fortunately, her healthcare expenses are covered by the military, so she doesn't need to budget for that. Life insurance is automatically deducted from her paycheck for Servicemembers Group Life Insurance (SGLI). She was automatically enrolled in a plan with $250,000 coverage for $18.50 per month. Since she has no dependents, she decides to drop her coverage to $100,000 for $8 per month, saving over $100 per year.[17] (Insurance is discussed in Chapter 6.)

Finally, our 2Lt realizes she should budget for plane tickets to visit her family over the holidays. She allows up to $500 for plane tickets, which comes out to $42 per month. She also plans for up to $300 per month for charity. After some quick math, she sees there is $380 left over, which she finds reasonable for entertainment purposes.

She has done it! She has $4,113 in post-tax monthly income, and her budgeted expenses just equal $4,113 per month (see budget on next page). She can live comfortably, save for retirement, and make ends meet. Of course, once she puts her budget into practice, she may have to make some adjustments. Now she just needs to figure out where to store her money throughout the month.

NOTE: This was a budget exercise originally intended for cadets at the Air Force Academy, so we used a new 2Lt. Most students right out of high school or college will not find it as easy to make a budget unless they find very good employment. Notice the 2Lt's annual income before taxes is $55,664, considerably more than the average income for a single person household shown in the BLS report, which was $33,487. Additionally, a good portion of the 2Lt's income is not taxed, making the disparity even greater (see Appendix A).

---

[17] http://www.benefits.va.gov/insurance/sgli.asp

Sample Budget:

Disposable Income		**$4,113**
Expenses		
Savings		$500
Rent	$1,200	
Utilities	$202	
Renter's insurance	$16	
Total Housing		$1,418
Food		$350
Car payment	$539	
Car insurance	$100	
Gas	$115	
Maintenance	$40	
Total Transportation		$794
Phone		$60
Cable + Internet		$50
Personal care		$34
Apparel		$67
Household furnishings		$110
Life insurance		$8
Charity		$300
Travel to family		$42
Entertainment		$380
Total Expenses		**$4,113**

Chapter 4. Banking

4.1. Why Use Banks?

At its core, a **bank** is a business that serves as an intermediary between people who save and those who borrow.[18] While there are legal differences between banks and credit unions, for our purposes we use the term "bank" to refer to both types of institutions. (The main difference is that a bank is a traditional business, either publicly or privately owned, while a **credit union** is owned by its customers, called members; so a credit union typically has lower fees and better rates than a bank.)

The main reason to use a bank is to have a safe place to keep your money. All deposits up to $250,000 are guaranteed by the Federal Deposit Insurance Corporation (FDIC).[19] (For credit unions, the insurance is provided by the National Credit Union Administration (NCUA).[20]). If the bank is robbed or goes out of business, depositors will still get their money back. The money you deposit is used by the bank to make loans to people and businesses looking to make large purchases (home and automobile purchases, factory expansion, etc.). Typically, a bank will pay interest to savers and charge a higher interest rate to borrowers. The bank makes money on the difference between those rates (as well as fees charged for other services).

Banks also provide several options for secure payment systems: personal checks, bank checks, and wire transfers. A **personal check** is a piece of paper you sign that authorizes a specific person to withdraw a specified amount of money from your account. It is secure because you can put a stop payment on a check that is lost, or you can close your account if your entire checkbook is lost. Also, if you need to prove that you made a payment, a cleared check appears on your bank statement. When the person or company you give the check to deposits the check, it is processed by the Federal Reserve (unless it is deposited into the same bank). The process has

---

[18] "Banking Basics," p6
[19] "Banking Basics," p34
[20] "How Your Accounts Are Federally Insured"

been electronic since 2004, but checks used to be physically mailed to the originating bank to be "cleared" (i.e., process the payment).[21] If the money was not available in the account, the check was stamped "NSF" (not sufficient funds) and "bounced" back to the sender. So a check is a secure form of payment for the payer, but not guaranteed to the payee. (Note, if you bounce a check, your bank will likely charge you a large fee ($35 to $50) and the company you wrote the check to may also charge you a fee. Don't bounce checks!)

A **bank check** is similar to a personal check, but the bank withdraws the money when the check is written so it is guaranteed to not bounce. A **wire transfer** skips the paper and transfers the money directly. While checks are becoming less necessary with the growth of online payment options and payment systems like PayPal and Venmo, it is still useful to understand how checks work. Section 4.3 explains how to write and read a check.

There are other services provided by banks, like ATMs, debit and credit cards, notaries, and investment services. Banks provide automatic teller machines (ATMs) that allow you to make deposits and withdrawals in more convenient locations, 24 hours a day. While ATMs are handy, you should be aware of fees that can be charged. Typically, a bank will charge fees if you use an ATM they do not own. The company that owns the ATM could also charge you a fee. You should be aware of these and stick to ATM machines that do not charge you, pick a bank that reimburses ATM fees, or manage your cash better to minimize the need to use ATMs. Consider this, if you have an average balance of $500 in your checking account, and access another bank's ATM every other week (paying a $2 fee), then over the course of a year you will pay $52 in fees. That's over 10% of your average balance! That is not good money management. If you saved that $52 every year in a tax-deferred retirement account earning an 8% return, over the course of 40 years you would accumulate more than $13,000 just from your savings on ATM fees.[22] Don't pay ATM fees!

---

[21] "Banking Basics," p24
[22] Excel formula "=FV(0.08,40,-52)" (see Appendix E)

Fees can also be a problem with bank-provided debit and credit cards, which are discussed in the next chapter.

A notary public is a person that legally witnesses signatures, which is frequently required for legal documents. Many banks provide this service free to customers. Many banks also offer investment management services, although these accounts are typically not insured. Chapters 7 and 8 discuss investments and retirement.

When choosing a bank, it is important to consider several factors:

- **Fees.** In addition to interest on loans, banks make money from fees charged to customers, typically to customers who don't pay attention and don't shop the competition. There can be account set up fees, monthly account fees, excessive check fees, ATM usage fees, bank teller usage fees, and more. Frequently, the fees are waived if you maintain a minimum balance in the account or if you establish electronic payroll deposits. It should not be too difficult to find a bank that provides free savings and checking accounts.

- **Convenience.** Before blindly signing up with the bank that has the lowest fees, you should be aware of the location and number of branches and ATMs available. You should also consider the banking hours and the availability of drive-through tellers and online services. Sometimes it is worth paying for convenience.

- **FDIC or NCUA insurance.** This should be automatic, but always verify deposit insurance before selecting a bank.

There are lots of options when it comes to banking. You must decide what best fits your lifestyle. Our recommendation, however, is to find an account somewhere with no fees for checking and no minimum balance–there are many banks and credit unions around that will do this, particularly if your paycheck is directly deposited there.

4.2. Types of Accounts

There are many types of accounts where you can store your money. Different accounts are better suited for different purposes. Are you saving for retirement? Then you should have a long-term, tax-deferred retirement account, such as an IRA or 401K account. Are you using the account for emergency savings? Then you will want a different account that has less risk and is readily accessible. Here is a brief explanation of some of the more common accounts you will find at a bank.

Short-Term, Easy-Access Accounts. These accounts are for convenience and **liquidity** (i.e., easily converted to cash)– accounts you use regularly to pay your bills. Because you want easy access to your funds, these accounts generally do not pay much interest. There is an opportunity cost: you gain liquidity, but earn very little income.

Checking Accounts. You probably already have a checking account through your bank or credit union. Checking accounts are "demand deposit" accounts– meaning the bank must give you access to your money in the account on demand. You access your money using checks, ATM machines, and debit cards. Here are a few things to consider:

- Does the account offer "free" checking, or do you have to pay a fee? It's hard to imagine why anyone would pay a fee today for a checking account. Back in the 1970s, many banks did charge fees for writing checks. No joke: banks charged ten cents per check. If your checking account charges you fees for normal usage, consider finding someplace else to do your banking.

- Does the account pay interest or require a minimum balance? A Negotiable Order of Withdrawal (NOW) account pays interest. This may seem like a sweet deal, but often these accounts require high minimum balances–and there's an opportunity cost to having a high minimum balance. NOW accounts may also charge larger fees if your balance drops below the minimum. If that happens, you could easily wipe out several years' worth of interest payments with a single fee.

Savings Accounts. Savings accounts are similar to checking accounts, except that they pay interest (minimal), may require a minimum balance (often small), and typically limit the number of times you can withdraw money from the account in a month. Savings accounts are FDIC-insured, just like checking accounts, and may be a reasonable choice for money you might need quickly (such as to pay insurance bills), but not necessarily on a daily basis. You earn a small amount of interest and have almost as much access to your money as in a checking account. The interest you earn in these accounts is taxable, just like any other regular income. It is convenient to have your savings account at the same bank as your checking account, so you can easily transfer funds between the two. But be careful about keeping too much money in a savings account; the opportunity cost is too high considering the unusually low interest rates paid on most savings accounts.

Money Market Accounts. These are like savings accounts on steroids. Money market accounts generally pay higher interest rates than savings accounts, but often have higher minimum balances as well (perhaps $1,000 or more). Like savings accounts, there usually are limits on how often you can withdraw money from a money market account without paying a service charge. Money market accounts are also FDIC insured at banks, just like checking and savings accounts. So, if you want to earn more interest on your "emergency" savings account, a money market account may be a better choice. (Note: Money market accounts offered by brokerage firms are typically money market mutual funds–and are not FDIC insured.)

To provide a concrete example to the discussion above, below are some details on checking accounts, savings accounts, and money market accounts offered by a large national bank, based on their website in January 2017. (We're not naming the bank or including the references so we don't appear biased for or against the bank, although we will say this is not the cheapest bank you can find.)

Free Checking Account

- Direct deposit is required (waived for students under age 23)
- No minimum balance, no service charge
- Unlimited check writing, free online banking, free bill payment
- Free transactions at bank-owned ATMs; $2.50 charge for transactions at other ATMs ($5 for overseas ATMs)
- No interest earned on deposits

Regular Checking Account

- No service charge with a minimum daily balance of $1,500
- If your balance is below the minimum for any day in a month, there is a $12 fee
- Unlimited check writing, free online banking, free bill payment.
- Free transactions at bank-owned ATMs; $2.50 charge for transactions at other ATMs ($5 for overseas ATMs)
- No interest earned on deposits.

Checking With Interest

- No service charge with an average daily balance of $10,000 (for all linked accounts)
- If your balance is below the average balances during a month, there is a $25 fee
- Unlimited check writing, free online banking, free bill payment.
- Free transactions at bank-owned ATMs; $2.50 charge for transactions at other ATMs ($5 for overseas ATMs)
- 0.01% to 0.03% interest earned (based on account balance)

Regular Savings

- No service charge with a minimum daily balance of $300
- If your balance is below the minimum balance during the month, there is a $5 fee
- Six withdrawals and transfers per month at no charge; $10 fee for each additional withdrawal or transfer
- 0.01% interest earned on account balance.

Money Market Account

- No service charge with a minimum daily balance of $2,500
- If your balance is below the minimum balance during the month, there is a $12 fee
- Six withdrawals and transfers per month at no charge; $10 fee for each additional withdrawal or transfer
- 0.03 to 0.06% interest on account balance is the current rate paid on a $1,000 balance.

A final note on fees: be sure to check ALL the details on your bank accounts. Frequently, a bank will offer nice-sounding items like overdraft protection, in which the bank will automatically transfer money from your savings account to your checking account to avoid an overdraft situation (i.e., a bounced check). While this sounds good, the bank may have a fee for this service (the bank used above charges $12 per transfer). That fee is probably better than the $35 overdraft fee (plus whatever the payee charges you), but it's better to not bounce checks to begin with. You do that by paying attention to your money.

Medium-Term Accounts. These accounts trade off the liquidity of short-term accounts for higher interest rates. These could be a good idea if you are saving for a specific purchase in the future, like a down payment on a home or a car.

Bank Certificates of Deposit (CD). You can usually earn a higher interest rate from your bank by putting your money in a CD. When you invest in a CD, it will have a designated period of time before it reaches maturity–this specifies how long you must keep your money deposited in the CD before you can withdraw it without incurring a penalty. Generally longer term CDs pay higher interest rates than short-term CDs, but not always. As an example, the table below shows the interest rates paid by our sample bank as of January 2017. (NOTE: interest rates are incredibly low in 2017. A 2007 column is included for comparison). APY means annual percentage yield and is explained in Appendix E.

Period	APY in 2017	APY in 2007
3 months	0.03%	3.25%
6 months	0.03%	4.50%
12 months	0.05%	5.05%
18 months	0.07%	5.15%
2 years	0.10%	4.90%
3 years	0.12%	4.50%
5 years	0.15%	4.25%

Like other bank accounts, CDs are usually FDIC insured, so your money is going to be there when you need it. But with a CD you forego the opportunity cost of investing your money in other potentially more lucrative investments while you wait for the CD to mature. Nevertheless, CDs may still be a reasonable choice to hold your money if you know that you must have access to your funds in six months or a year. However, as a long-term investment for your kids' education, your retirement fund, or saving for your dream home, there are other alternatives that have historically paid better returns over the long run.

Long-Term Accounts. If you do not need immediate access to your money, there are ways to earn better returns, although in addition to less liquidity, you're also exposing yourself to more risk. Chapter 8 will review different types of investment vehicles, and Chapter 7 will discuss retirement options, which add the benefit of tax-deferred or tax-free earnings.

4.3. Checks

As discussed earlier, a check is just a piece of paper that authorizes the payee to withdraw a specified amount of money from the account of the payer. There are many different types and styles of checks, but the sample below is fairly representative of what you can expect to see on any check.

```
Wile E. Coyote                                        0123
123 Any St
Sometown, CO 80841              1/11/17
                                                      Date

Pay to the    ACME Industries
order of                                      $    95 00

Ninety-five  00/100                                Dollars

AnyBank
888 Main  St
Bigtown, FL 32611

Memo   Roadrunner trap              W. E. Coyote

 :012345678:  01234567890123   0123
```

Routing number   Account number   Check number

Payer. This is the name and address of the account holder from whom funds are transferred. In this case, it is a check from Wile E. Coyote.

Payee. This is the name of the person or company that is being authorized to take the money. The name is written on the "Pay to the order of" line. In this case, the payee is ACME Industries.

Date. The date the check is written goes in the upper right portion of the check. While there is no legal expiration date for checks, firms and banks typically list an expiration anywhere from as little as 60 days to as much as one year from the date on the check.

Amount. The check amount must be shown both numerically in the box and written out on the line below. These amounts must match or the bank may refuse to pay.

Bank. The bank information is printed below the written amount. There are no set rules for how much bank information is required. The more important information is along the bottom of the check, which includes the **routing number** (specific to the bank), the payer's account number, and the check number. Some checks also include a bank identification number (different from the routing number) in the upper right portion of the check near the date. (Our sample does not have a bank ID.)

Memo. This is a blank space where you can write anything. It is usually used to write notes to yourself on what the check was for. When writing checks to pay bills, you should include your account number or invoice number (listed on the bill) in this area.

Signature. A check must be signed by the payer. Depending on how thorough the bank wants to be, this signature must match the account holder's signature card on file with the bank.

After writing a check (or using your debit card or any transaction that affects your checking account), you should immediately record it in your checkbook's **register**. That's a paper booklet that comes with your checks to help you track the balance of your checking account. (You could also track it with a spreadsheet, which makes it easier to search for things in the future.) The advent of electronic banking and phone apps to check up-to-the-minute account balances makes many people think you don't need to use a register, but realize that checks you've written that still haven't cleared are not reflected on your account, so the balance you see on your phone app may not be the funds you actually have available. Keeping track of the transactions yourself is the best way to avoid over- drawing your account.

NUMBER	DATE	CODE	DESCRIPTION OF TRANSACTION	PAYMENT/DEBIT(-)		FEE(-)	TAX	DEPOSIT/CREDIT(+)		$	723.45
0122	12/24		Nature Pets	44	30						
			Grooming							679	15
	12/26	D	Cash deposit					100	00		
			Gift from mom							779	15
	12/30	DC	XYZ Party Supply	33	67						
			Balloons and hats							743	48
123	1/11		ACME Industries	95	00						
			Roadrunner trap							648	48

A typical register is shown above. The first column is to track check numbers. For other transactions (deposits, automatic payments, debit card transactions, etc.), you can leave it blank. The date is self-explanatory. Some registers have a column for a code to distinguish transaction types. For example, DC for debit card, D for deposit, AP for automatic payment, ATM for automatic teller withdrawals, etc. The description column allows you to not only write who the payment went to, but also has space to include the purpose. The columns for payment/debit and fee both have minus signs on them because these are things to deduct from the previous row's balance. (If you're doing things right, you should never have a fee on your checking account.) Some registers will have a tax column to allow you to track items you may need to refer back to for tax purposes in the future. The deposit/credit column has a plus sign because this is added to the previous row's balance. The final column is for the account balance after the transaction clears.

Of course, if you forget to record automatic payments or debit card transactions in your check register, the balance here will not be any more reliable than the balance on your phone app that does not account for uncleared checks. As with any other system that tracks data, the quality of the information is only as good as the quality of what you put into it. If you're keeping track of your budget on a spreadsheet, it should not be too much additional effort to track your account balance with a spreadsheet. This will keep you from getting into trouble. It is also useful to look into the future. If you're tracking your account with a spreadsheet, you can easily copy and paste the previous month to forecast the next month and see what happens to your balance. If it's getting smaller, you may have some adjustments to make. If it is consistently getting larger, you have an opportunity to increase your savings rate.

Finally, suppose someone writes a check to you. What do you do with it? You have to **endorse** the check in order to claim the money. That is, you have to sign on the back (where it says "Endorse check here", on the top third of the back of the check). The signature must match the name as written on the front and once you sign it, the check can be cashed by anyone. It is safer to do a restrictive endorsement by including a statement under your signature. For example, you can write "for deposit only" or "deposit into account no. #####" in order to ensure the check can only be deposited into your account. If you want to endorse it over to someone in particular, you can add "pay to the order of John Doe," and then only John Doe can cash the check.

Chapter 5. Credit

5.1. What is Credit?

Credit really just means borrowing. Essentially you're trading your reputation as a promise to repay a loan. Of course, firm's don't loan money for free. The cost of borrowing is typically measured by the interest rate you must pay, but that can be deceiving because rates are not always the same. The frequency of interest charges can greatly change how much you actually pay (see the difference between APR and APY in Appendix E). Also, there can be other costs to taking a loan (origination, closing, credit checks, etc.). You should be clear on what you're getting into before taking a loan because costs can be exorbitant (especially at payday loan shops).

When you borrow money, the loan can be secured or unsecured. In a **secured loan**, there is some asset at stake that the creditor can take if you fail to pay as promised. Examples include mortgages (for real estate) and car loans. Because of the collateral, secured loans typically have lower interest rates and easier approval than unsecured loans. Examples of **unsecured loans** include student loans, bank lines of credit, and credit cards. Even with a secured loan, your approval and cost (interest rate) are dependent on your reputation as reflected in your credit score.

There are many specific types of debt. We're only going to cover credit cards and basic simple interest loans used for mortgages and car loans. Before getting into those specifics, some basics on debt and credit scores are needed.

5.2. Good vs Bad Debt

While credit is convenient, it is not free money and can get you into a lot of financial trouble if you over-extend yourself. It is important to consider why you would want to go into debt. Businesses go into debt in order to leverage limited financial assets and earn larger returns. For example, suppose a firm can purchase a $100,000 piece of equipment that increases profits by $10,000. That is a $10,000/$100,000 = 10\% return on investment. Now suppose the firm could finance the equipment, paying $20,000 the first year. In that scenario, the firm's return is $10,000/$20,000 = 50\% (in the first year). It's not always this cut and dried, but firms always consider the internal rate of return (IRR) of projects in order to determine if they exceed their average cost of capital (i.e., the interest rates they pay on loans).

The decision to acquire individual debt is rarely that straightforward. What's the IRR for a house or a college education? You may not be able to quantify those benefits, but you can easily quantify the cost of the loans. You need to consider whether the benefits of the debt exceed the costs. Generally debt is OK if you are using it for an appreciating asset (like a house). Still, you want to follow the general rules of thumb:

- Keep housing debt $< 28\%$ of your income
- Keep total debt $< 36\%$ of your income

Obviously, less debt is better than more debt, but there are also qualities of debt. You do not want to go into debt for depreciating assets (consumer goods, appliances, etc.). Some would include cars here, but one of your authors is a self-professed car snob. Besides, most people rarely have enough money saved up to buy a big-ticket item like a car early in their lives. Housing and transportation purchases are discussed in Chapter 9.

You definitely do not want to go into debt for consumable goods because you'll have nothing to show for the debt when the bills are due. There are genuine emergencies when this may be necessary, but generally, if you are going into debt like this, you are probably living beyond your means.

5.3. Establishing Good Credit

There is no shortage of companies and internet sites offering to report or improve your credit. You should be wary of these sites if you are not familiar with the firms because they frequently charge you for things you can get for free, and/or they ask for a lot of personal information that could expose you to identity theft (which many claim to help prevent). Your bank may be able to provide you with a credit report, so there may be no need to involve another firm. Also, the three largest credit reporting firms in the U.S. (Experian, TransUnion, and Equifax) banded together to create a site which allows you to get a free credit report every 12 months.[23] If in doubt, you can get more specific credit information from the Consumer Financial Protection Bureau at www.consumerfinance.gov.

All the credit reporting firms (or credit bureaus) assign a **credit score** based on your credit history. The score is a proprietary formula, based on your credit report, which is supposed to predict how likely you are to pay your debts as promised. The **credit report** includes any information about your borrowing habits and may include:[24]

- A list of businesses that have given you credit or loans
- The total amount for each loan or credit limit for each credit card
- How often you paid your credit or loans on time, and the amount you paid
- Any missed or late payments, as well as bad debts
- A list of businesses that have obtained your credit report within a certain time period
- Your current and former names, address(es) and/or employers
- Any bankruptcies or other public record information

The better your credit score, the easier your access to credit and the lower your rates will be. Also, you may find other things in life are related to your credit score, such as insurance premiums and even your employability.[25] So how do you improve your credit score? Without knowing the exact formula a credit bureau uses, it's difficult to know for certain, but the basic rule is _always pay your bills on time_. The Consumer Financial

---

[23] www.annualcreditreport.com
[24] "All About Credit Reports." Annualcreditreport.com
[25] Employers cannot pull your credit score, but they can pull a credit report

Protection Bureau has these suggestions to improve your credit score:[26]

- Pay your bills on time
- Don't get too close to your credit limit (i.e., don't max out your credit cards)
- Don't apply for too much credit in a short time
- Pay your credit card balance every month
- Check your credit reports and fix errors right away

Sometimes people say you should cut up your credit cards to help control your spending. That may not apply anymore since your card information is probably stored in any online stores you've used. In order to truly remove the temptation to spend, you have to actually cancel the account, not just cut up the card. However, closing the account could hurt your credit score by increasing your **credit utilization**.[27] That is the amount of debt you hold as a percent of the total credit you have available. As Brownell explains, if you have two cards with $10,000 limits and carry a total debt of $8,000, your credit utilization is $8,000/$20,000 = 40\%$. If you transfer the balance to a single card and cancel the other one, your credit utilization doubles. You have the same debt but appear riskier on a credit report. Your focus should be on paying down that debt to improve your credit score and avoid the interest charges on those credit cards.

Sometimes credit becomes a chicken and egg problem. How do you establish good credit if you need good credit to qualify for credit? The best way to establish credit is to have a family member co-sign on a loan or credit card to get approval. Another option is to get a secured credit card from your bank. For a secured credit card, you set aside an amount of cash equivalent to the card's credit limit. That way, your bank is guaranteed to not be stuck with your bad debt. If you make all your scheduled payments for some period of time (typically a year), the bank will refund your deposit and the card will transition to a regular unsecured credit card. It seems like a silly idea. Why put aside money to borrow money? Sadly, that may

---

[26] "How to Rebuild Your Credit."
[27] Brownell

be your only option to help start your credit history. The sooner you start, the better your score will be in the future.

Military members have it much easier when establishing credit because creditors know a lot about their employment and compensation. Also, the Uniform Code of Military Justice (UCMJ) specifically address debt issues, which can be cause for a dishonorable discharge. Prior to 2013, military commanders could assist creditors in extracting payment from military members.[28] While this is no longer allowed, creditors still view military members as less risky when extending credit.

5.4. Credit Cards

Credit cards can be very convenient. You don't have to carry cash, and you get monthly statements to help track your expenses. There's also added security when using a credit card. When you use a debit card, the bank is not loaning you money. The money is withdrawn from your account and deposited in the store's account. So if you don't have the money in your account, you can't use your debit card (the transaction will be declined or you'll be hit with an overdraft fee). In addition, since debit card payments are taken directly out of your checking account, someone who steals your debit card could potentially wipe out all of the money in your checking account. In contrast, credit cards usually have a fairly low liability for loss (e.g., $50) if you notify your credit card company immediately after finding out the card was stolen or lost. Also, many credit cards come with perks like cash back, airline miles, extended warranties, etc... just make sure they don't come with any fees.

Most credit cards work the same way. The issuer makes money from both ends of a transaction. They typically charge the seller a fee based on the purchase price (2-3%). The fee is justified because the credit card company is taking the risk of a consumer defaulting (versus the seller if they took a personal check). Also, the credit card company is facilitating the transaction by allowing consumers to just carry a piece of

---

[28] 2015 Commander's Legal Handbook, p295

plastic and not worry about carrying large sums of cash (especially for larger purchases). On the consumer side, credit card companies make money by charging annual fees (in some cases) and charging interest on outstanding balances.

You should be able to find a credit card that does not charge an annual fee. If yours currently does, you need to start shopping around for a better card. You also should not be paying interest on your credit card because you should be using it for convenience, not to live beyond your means. As long as you pay the statement balance each month, most credit card companies offer a grace period with no interest on new purchases until the next billing cycle. However, if you do not pay the full balance, the credit company will likely start charging interest immediately on the remaining balance and all new purchases. Also, credit cards usually compound interest on a daily basis so the actual rate you pay is much higher than the stated APR on the card.

Personally, we're not too concerned with the rate that a credit card charges because you shouldn't be carrying a balance on the card (so you won't pay interest). It's most important to look for a card that has no annual fee. Additional perks like cash back are nice, but only if you can get them without an annual fee.

5.5. Mortgages and Car Loans

Most secured bank loans for houses and cars are simple interest loans. Each month, interest is charged on the balance of the loan, but once the full amount is paid, there are no more interest charges. That means there is no penalty for repaying the loan early (although you should always verify this when taking out a loan). Typically, these loans set a rate based on the duration of the loan (36 to 60 months for cars; 15 to 30 years for houses), with higher rates for longer loans.

Let's look at an example to see how these loans work. Suppose you borrow $20,000 at 6% annual percentage rate (APR) on a 48 month car loan. The required minimum payment each month will be $469.70.[29] The interest is compounded monthly, so you're being charged 6%/12 = 0.5% each month. When you make the first payment, you owe $20,000 x 0.005 = $100 in interest. Therefore, only $469.70 – $100 = $369.70 pays down the loan (i.e., is applied to principal), and your balance owed is $20,000 – $369.70 = $19,630.30 after the first payment. The next month, your interest charge will be $19,630.30 x 0.005 = $98.15. The table below shows the first few months of payments. (You should verify these numbers to see if you grasp the concept.)

Month	Balance	Interest	Principal
1	$20,000.00	$100.00	$369.70
2	$19,630.30	$98.15	$371.55
3	$19,258.75	$96.29	$373.41
4	$18,885.34	$94.43	$375.27
5	$18,510.07	$92.55	$377.15

If you pay more than the minimum payment, all of the additional payment would go to paying down the principal. Your required minimum payment will not change, but your future interest charges will be less, making more of your future payments go toward paying down the principal. If you pay an extra $100 each month, the loan will be completely repaid in 39 months, rather than 48. This is a technique frequently recommended to repay mortgages faster.

Speaking of mortgages, there are many other flavors of mortgages: adjustable-rate mortgages (ARM), zero-down mortgages, interest-only mortgages. Some of these can be useful if you know what you're getting into. They can also be very dangerous, as evidenced by the housing market crash in 2008. Many people found themselves "underwater" on their mortgages. That is, the value of their home was less than the amount owed on the loan. In other words, they couldn't sell their house without having to pay money out of pocket. That is a terrible situation. They likely got there by taking advantage of zero-down mortgages that allowed them to pay interest only in the first couple of years. The benefit of such a mortgage is that you can get a lower monthly payment and buy more house than

[29] Excel formula "=PMT(.06/12,48,-20000)" (see Appendix E)

you could otherwise afford. (Another possibility is that they had a very low down payment, so they owed a large percentage of the value of the house, and then the house's value dropped rapidly, below the amount they owed.) If you plan to sell quickly and property values are appreciating, such a loan could be a good investment. When property values crash, however, you get caught with the hot potato and you can be ruined financially.

To avoid these risks, we recommend sticking with a conventional, fixed-rate mortgage and abiding by the tried-and-true practice of not buying a house until you can make a 20% down payment. That is not a requirement, but it's a good rule of thumb. Also, having over 80% equity in the home means you are not forced to buy mortgage insurance or pay into an **escrow account**. An escrow account is used to collect money for property taxes and homeowners insurance, which are then paid when due by the escrow agent. This is to protect your mortgage lender from losing its investment in your home should you fail to pay the taxes yourself. The problem with an escrow account is that you lose control of the money (so you can't keep it yourself in an interest-bearing account). Also, if you're not paying attention to the payments, you may not have the best prices or plan for your homeowners insurance. Worse, if the escrow agent misses a tax payment, you may not know about it until it's too late. See Chapter 9 for more home buying tips.

Chapter 6. Retirement Plans

Other than having a checking account and a nominal amount of savings for an emergency, probably the first thing most experts recommend is that you start socking away some money for your retirement. There are three reasons you should start saving for retirement early:

1. Compounding
2. Tax-deferred
3. Wrong generation

First, the power of compound interest is amazing. Start early if you want to have a big impact. Let's look at an example. Consider Mr. Smart and Mr. Delay. We'll assume both are equally adept investors, and earn a constant 10% on their investments until retirement. However, Mr. Smart begins saving $3,000 per year at the age of 21, right after graduating from college. In contrast, Mr. Delay waits 10 years, until he is 31 years old, to start saving for his retirement, but he saves twice as much per year ($6,000) to catch up. If Mr. Smart puts away $3,000 per year through his 61st birthday, he will have saved a total of $3,000 x 40 years = $120,000 out of his paychecks. Meanwhile, Mr. Delay took $6,000 x 30 years = $180,000 from his paychecks. Since Mr. Delay had to take 50% more out of his paychecks, you might think he will have more money when he retires, but he won't. Mr. Smart has the better retirement, because his investment compounded over a longer period of time. In fact, when they each turn 61 years old, the amount each will have on hand in his retirement account is:

Mr. Smart's Account Value at Age 61 = $1,460,555

Mr. Delay's Account Value at Age 61 = $1,085,661

Mr. Smart took $60,000 *less* out of his paychecks, but has almost $400,000 more in his retirement account because he started early! Do not delay saving for retirement. Appendix E explains how to do these types of calculations.[30]

---

[30] We are using standard financial calculations with the *average* returns (shown in Appendix E). This ignores the *variability* (or risk) in the return, so it's almost guaranteed to be wrong. That's OK for our purposes here. For more realistic

The second reason you should begin saving early for retirement is because the government allows certain types of retirement accounts to grow tax-deferred. That means the money you invest is not taxed until you begin withdrawing the money after retirement. Some experts say that is important because you'll probably be in a lower tax bracket after retirement so you'll pay fewer taxes on your investment. That may be true, but it still misses the biggest benefit of tax-deferral, which is the much larger amount of wealth accumulation you'll have because you aren't paying taxes while the money in your account is compounding. Let's use Mr. Smart as our example once again. Suppose Mr. Smart has his retirement account in an IRA or some other tax-deferred account, and he earns an average of 10% return on his investments throughout his life. As we showed above, Mr. Smart will have $1,460,555 in his retirement account when he turns 61. In contrast, suppose his buddy, Mr. Lagg, follows the same savings plan ($3,000 per year beginning at age 21), but Mr. Lagg puts his money in an account which is not tax-deferred. Even though Mr. Lagg also earns 10% per year on his investment, every year the government takes 20% of Mr. Lagg's investment return in income taxes. Thus, while the gross return on Mr. Lagg's investment is 10% annually, his net return is just 8% on his investment. So when both investors reach the ripe age of 61 they will each have the following amounts:

Mr. Smart's Account Value at Age 61 = $1,460,555

Mr. Lagg's Account Value at Age 61 = $839,343

Because Mr. Lagg did not take advantage of the tax-deferred status of a retirement account, he has amassed $600,000 less than Mr. Smart—even though they both invested the same total amount of their paychecks for 40 years. Now, you may be thinking, "but what about the taxes Mr. Smart owes on his tax-

---

results, you can simulate the returns and derive a distribution for the expected portfolio value. For example, an investment with average return of 10% and standard deviation of 20% will see returns at −22% or worse 5% of the time. After 5,000 trials, the portfolio value for Mr. Smart ranged from $71,000 (catastrophic losses) to $16M, but the average was still $1.46M and the chance of losing money was only 0.1%. Mr. Smart's portfolio value beat Mr. Delay's value 70% of the time. For more information see Section E6 or read *The Flaw of Averages* by Sam Savage.

deferred account when he withdraws the money?" Good point. But remember, he's likely to pay a lower tax rate in retirement—and even if he pays 20% on his entire investment, he still ends up with more than $1.1 million after taxes. No matter how you look at it, tax-deferred retirement accounts have a huge advantage over taxable accounts. (Oh yes—and if Mr. Smart is invested in a Roth IRA, he will not even have to pay taxes on his withdrawal after retirement!)

Finally, we hate to bring this up, but the truth is that you picked a bad year to be born (with regard to Social Security). Social Security was created in 1935 to provide an income for the old and poor of America.[31] It is managed so that the social security taxes of current workers are used to pay the benefits of the currently retired. The social security taxes you are paying today are being used to pay retirement benefits for your grandparents. When you are retired, your grandchildren will be working (hopefully) and making contributions to pay for your benefits. The problem is that people are living a lot longer today than in 1935 and having fewer children. This means there are more retired people and fewer workers per retiree to pay their benefits. Simply put, there will not be enough young people working and making contributions to cover the cost of your retirement—at least not at the level the government is currently promising. Here is what the Social Security Administration's Board of Trustees said about the system in their 2016 Annual Report:[32]

> The Trustees also project that annual cost for the OASDI program will exceed non-interest income throughout the projection period, and will exceed total income beginning in 2020 under the intermediate assumptions. The projected hypothetical combined OASI and DI Trust Fund asset reserves increase through 2019, begin to decline in 2020, and become depleted and unable to pay scheduled benefits in full on a timely basis in 2034.

This is not new information. In the 2007 report, the Board of Trustees projected fund would be depleted in 2041, so the

---

[31] See Social Security History at www.ssa.gov/history/history.html
[32] "2016 Report of the Board of Trustees," p6

system is actually getting worse.[33] There is the possibility that changes will be made to keep the system solvent, but you can expect to pay higher taxes and to receive fewer benefits. So we recommend you don't count on Social Security to bail you out in retirement.

The rest of this chapter will discuss different types of retirement plans, which are essentially special tax treatments for investments. Actual types of investments will be discussed in the next chapter. Most of the limits and numbers included will quickly be outdated. You can find up-to-date numbers easily by searching the irs.gov website.

Before starting, realize there are two basic types of retirement plans: **individual plans** (where you do it yourself) and **employer plans** (where your employer sets it up for you, usually through a third party). Within employer plans, there are two types: pensions and investment plans. A pension, or **defined-benefit plan**, provides a specified amount of money per year based on factors leading up to your retirement (such as number of years employed and salary earned). An investment plan, or **defined-contribution plan**, has specified amounts your employer will contribute (typically based on what you contribute), but the value of the plan when you retire is based on what you chose to do with the money. That is, what types of investments you put the money into. Clearly, the latter plan is preferred by most employers because there is no uncertainty. With lifespans increasing, defined-benefit plans are very expensive, so most employers have moved to defined-contribution plans, like 401(k)s. The military retirement system discussed in Appendix A is an example of a defined-benefit plan.

There are many types of retirement plans, including pension profit-sharing or stock bonus plans (IRS tax code section 401(a)), qualified employee annuity plans (403(a)), tax-sheltered annuity plans (403(b)), and deferred compensation plans (457). We will only discuss the most common types: individual retirement accounts (or arrangements) and 401(k) plans.

---

[33] "2007 Report of the Board of Trustees," p2

6.1. Individual Retirement Accounts (IRAs)

The Employee Retirement Income Security Act of 1974 created the traditional IRA to enable and encourage individuals to save for retirement in tax-deferred accounts.[34] The Taxpayer Relief Act of 1997 created the Roth IRA.[35] By 2004, 40% of all households owned an IRA account, which collectively totaled more than $3 trillion dollars.[36] IRAs are truly a wonderful way to save for your retirement.

Traditional IRAs. The traditional IRA allows you to put *pre-tax* dollars into a *tax-deferred* retirement account. That is, you can deduct the money you invest in a traditional IRA in order to reduce your current taxable income. Suppose you are in the 15% marginal tax bracket. If you were to make a $4,000 contribution to your IRA, you could claim a $4,000 deduction on your income tax return. So you would essentially pay $4,000 x 0.15 = $600 less in taxes for the year because of this IRA deduction. That's a pretty sweet deal. On top of that, the money you put in your traditional IRA account could grow and grow, and you would not have to pay taxes on it until you withdrew the money at retirement.

Be aware, however, that there are fairly low income limits on making deductible contributions to traditional IRAs, and there are strings attached. In 2016, a single person making more than $71,000 per year or a married couple earning more than $118,000 per year could not make deductible contributions to a traditional IRA (if they were also covered by a retirement plan at work).[37] The contribution limit is $5,500 per person. Also, if you withdraw money before age 59 ½, you have to pay an additional 10% tax penalty, but you must start withdrawing money by age 70 ½ (by completing a form to determine your requirement minimum distribution).[38]

Roth IRAs. A Roth IRA differs from the traditional IRA because you save *after-tax* dollars into a *tax-free* retirement account. So,

---

[34] Holden, et.al., p1
[35] Lyke, p7
[36] Holden, et.al., pp1-2
[37] IRS Pub 590-A, p2
[38] IRS Pub 590-B, p6

if you put $4,000 into a Roth IRA, you don't save the $600 like you would with the traditional IRA. However, the great benefit on Roth IRA accounts is that once you make the contribution, your account can grow and grow and, in most cases, you never have to pay taxes on the money. This means your Roth IRA could grow to a million dollars, and when you begin withdrawing the money after retirement, you don't have to pay any taxes on your withdrawals either.

Like traditional IRAs, the Roth IRA also has contribution limits. For 2016, a married couple could not make a Roth contribution if their income exceeded $194,000, and a single person could not make a Roth contribution if income exceeded $132,000.[39] The contribution limit is the same, $5,500 per person. Another benefit of Roth IRAs is that there are generally fewer forms to fill out and less paperwork and record keeping to do, largely because the money is not taxed when you retire, so you don't have to keep track of your contributions into the account.

There are many debates about whether the traditional or the Roth IRA is the best investment. The debates get very detailed based on your current income level, your projected income streams in retirement, etc. Let us make it easy–get a Roth IRA. For most people a Roth IRA makes more sense and is simpler.

6.2. 401(k) Plans

You've probably heard friends and family talk about 401(k) plans for their retirement. This is just a retirement plan named after Section 401(k) of the Internal Revenue Service tax code– which is where these "tax-qualified deferred compensation" plans are addressed. A 401(k) plan is one in which an employee elects to have a portion of his *pre-tax* wage paid into a retirement plan directly by his employer, rather than having the employer pay him (and thereby incur income taxes).[40] It's kind of like a traditional IRA in that the employee gets to have some money set aside for retirement for which he doesn't have to pay income taxes, then that retirement account can grow tax-

---

[39] IRS Pub 590-A, p2
[40] IRS Pub 525, p9

deferred until you start withdrawing the funds at retirement. 401(k) plans are also portable, so when an employee leaves one company, he can transfer the funds in his 401(k) account to his new employer's 401(k) plan and continue saving for retirement.

One of the truly great deals in many 401(k) plans is that employers often "match" the contributions of the employee up to a specified limit. A company may pay 10 cents for every dollar the employee contributes, up to the first 10% of her income. That means she gets an immediate 10% return on her investment. Another company may offer a 100% match up to 3% of income. If your employer offers a 401(k), make sure you know the benefits so you can take full advantage.

6.3. Annuities

Just say no! Perhaps we're being a little too harsh, but we have yet to find any independent financial guidebook that recommends annuities as a good investment. An annuity is basically like a specialized insurance contract (see Chapter 8). You pay the insurance company up front when you are young and working, then after you retire, the insurance company (or whoever is holding the annuity) pays you back in either a lump sum or a stream of income payments. Like other retirement accounts, annuities generally grow tax-deferred, but there are a number of characteristics of annuities that make them poor investment choices. They generally charge high commissions (even if you don't see them listed in the contract). They historically have been poorly performing investments, and they often have large "surrender charges," which are fees the company imposes if you try to cash the annuity in too soon (which could be up to fifteen years from the time you purchase the annuity).[41]

Even though annuities are tax-deferred, when you withdraw money from your annuity, it may be taxed at the same rate as regular income rather than the lower, long-term capital gains rate you pay on most other long-term investments. Besides, the

---

[41] Opdyke, p196

tax-deferred status of an annuity is sort of irrelevant, because your IRA and 401(k) retirement plans are already tax-deferred and give you much greater investment flexibility than an annuity.

If you're still not convinced to avoid purchasing an annuity, consider the annuity advice offered by three other respectable personal finance guidebooks:

> "Most investors are better off without an annuity and should simply stick with mutual funds."
> – Jeff Opdyke, *The Wall Street Journal Complete Personal Finance Guidebook*, p194.

> "Consider contributing to an annuity only after you exhaust contributions to all your available retirement accounts."
> – Eric Tyson, *Personal Finance for Dummies*, p250.

> "Don't buy them!"
> – Andrew Tobias, *The Only Investment Guide You'll Ever Need*, p117.

Chapter 7. Investing

All of the retirement plans in the previous chapter are simply tax treatments, but they do not specify how to invest your money. Most of them give you many options. An IRA is an "account" but you can invest the money in stocks, bonds, mutual funds, and a variety of other investments. Inevitably, students want to know what's the best stock to pick or the best mutual fund, or other similar advice. While we can't tell you what the best individual investment is (it depends on your goals and attitudes towards risk), we can offer some advice on what types of investments have historically performed the best over the long run.

WARNING: This is the longest chapter in the book because we want to clearly explain our rationale for the advice at the end of the chapter. You may not be interested in the *why* and only care about *which* type of investment you should pick (in our opinion). If that's the case, you should skip to the "Our Advice" section at the end of the chapter. If you're genuinely interested in different types of investments (or are being forced to read about them for class), this chapter is for you. But before we talk about individual investments, let's first talk about the differences between investing and saving and give you warnings about brokers, financial advisors, and the like.

7.1. Investing vs. Saving

We used the term savings three times already, but we were not always talking about same thing. The original mentions of savings (Chapters 1 and 3) included all types of money you set aside for your own use later in life. This comprises both savings and investments. While this distinction may seem like splitting hairs, it is very important to differentiate the purpose of the money and how you plan to treat it based on your objectives.

When not used generally, savings (Chapter 4) specifically means money set aside for **preservation of capital**. That is, you want to maintain the value of your money while keeping up with inflation, but not risk losing any money. Savings should be invested into "safe" places like savings accounts, money market accounts, and even bonds and stable, dividend-paying stocks. You also want to maintain relatively easy access to the money in the short-term, either for planned purchases or for emergency expenses. That is, your savings should have high **liquidity** (a fancy way to say it is easily converted to cash).

The purpose of investing is **capital growth**. That is, you want returns on your money that exceed inflation in order to take advantage of compounding. As with savings, there are several avenues to pursue: stocks, mutual funds, real estate, and more. Generally, the riskier the investment, the greater the chance for faster growth (but higher risk also means a greater chance of losing money, so you need to be ready for that).

What proportion of your general savings you divert to savings versus investments depends on your goals and your situation in life. For younger people, once they have an emergency fund filled up, we would expect the majority of their savings to go into fairly aggressive investments to grow their nest egg as fast as possible. As people age, they should transition into safer investments and more savings in order to preserve the nest egg for retirement.

However you choose to do it, investing should be considered a long-term endeavor. If you are looking for immediate returns (i.e., day trading), that is no different than gambling. We're not saying not to do it, but just like going to Vegas, you should only do so if you're willing to lose the money. If you find day trading to be an exciting hobby, there's no problem with doing it for fun, but not as a part of your investment strategy. If you do it, set aside a specific amount of money for it and transition your gains immediately to safer investments to keep from losing it all.

7.2. Brokers & Advisors

Brokerage firms come in many different flavors, offering a range of services, at a vast range of different costs. Brokers at the traditional "full-service" firms call their clients to provide investment advice–tips on stocks to buy or sell, etc. In contrast, "discount" brokers do not contact clients directly, but simply offer the service of buying and selling stocks at a reduced fee. Of course, the line between discount brokerage firms and full-service firms is a little fuzzy. While a discount broker is unlikely to call you on the phone to offer advice, you can still obtain tremendous amounts of information about companies and stocks on your own simply by visiting the online research portion of the discount broker's website, or any number of other websites that offer online stock research—often for free.

It's really your call as to the kind of relationship you want to have with your broker—and what kind of fees you are willing to pay for your broker's advice. However, we want to offer just a few words of advice. First, be aware that full-service broker fees can be substantial—so if your broker is calling you and pushing you to buy a stock, that stock better perform extremely well, because the broker's sales commission is going to be higher than the purchase fee you will pay if you buy the stock yourself through a discount firm. Second, you should know *incentives matter.* There are two worries here. First, the broker might be calling you and recommending you purchase stock XYZ or bond XYZ because his brokerage firm has a financial arrangement itself with company XYZ that compels the brokers to make a hard sell. Second, most brokers earn commissions for buying and selling stocks—they make money on the trade, regardless of whether the stock goes up or down. Andrew Tobias is a little more frank in his evaluation of broker advice when he says, "Never buy anything from a broker who calls you up cold. This is so basic as not to warrant elaboration."[42]

Brokers have an incentive to convince you to frequently buy and sell stocks (paying them a hefty commission in the process), but the real wisdom on Wall Street is that smart investors make money by buying value investments and holding them for a long time while they appreciate. Frequently trading stocks, bonds, or other investments is an almost sure way to lose money in the market. Every time you make a trade, you have to pay a fee, shrinking your gains and amplifying your losses. So, we believe for most investors the best choice is some kind of discount broker. There are many discount brokers out there—Scottrade, Ameritrade, E*Trade, Fidelity, Vanguard,

---

[42] Tobias, p174

and Schwab, to name a few. Thanks to competition, the transaction fees at these discount brokers have fallen over the last ten years or so. A "cheap" trade used to be around $20, but many advertise trades around $7 now.

Of course, you may also enter into an arrangement with a financial advisor instead of with a broker to do your investing. Here again the line is often fuzzy, but in theory a financial advisor is governed by different rules than a broker. Brokers are supposed to offer clients "suitable" investments (which is almost impossible to define), while financial advisors are supposed to "put the client's needs first."[43] In reality, it can be difficult to tell the two apart in terms of the advice they give, but there are often differences in how they operate and bill you. A broker cannot buy or sell investments without your permission, whereas some advisory accounts give the financial advisor permission to trade on your behalf, without requiring your consent on each and every purchase or sale. Broker's generally earn their income on the trade itself–charging a fee for each sale or purchase. Financial advisors often charge a fee based on the size of your account, regardless of whether a trade is made. So, for example, a broker may charge you $40 to sell stock XYZ. On the other hand, a financial advisor may make the sale of stock XYZ on your behalf through a discount broker at a cost of $9 (of which the financial advisor earns nothing), but the advisor charges you an annual fee of 1% on the total amount of investments he handles for you in your accounts. (So, if your account is worth $50,000, then you would pay your financial advisor $500 per year to manage your account–irrespective of the number of trades).

Which is better? That's a tough call that really depends on the individual broker or financial advisor. But, unless you have a special connection with a person who has a demonstrated ability to consistently beat the market with his advice, you should probably just find a discount broker. Why is that? Because after you account for their commission costs and fees, ***studies have consistently shown that the majority of brokers and financial planners underperform the market***. That means you're paying for advice that is frequently worth

---

[43] Opdyke, p84

less than a purely random stock pick. Andrew Tobias makes this point a bit more eloquently by writing the following:

> *There are no brokers who can beat the market consistently and by enough of a margin to more than make up for their brokerage fees. Or, if there are a few, they are not going to work for peanuts–and any account under $500,000 is peanuts. Or if they will—because they are just starting out in business or have a soft spot in their heart for you—there's no way to know who they are. Even if they have done well in the past (not just say it—prove it), that doesn't mean they will do very well in the future.*
>
> *If you get 256 people into a room and give them each a coin to flip, the odds are that half of them–128—will flip heads on the first try. That is the object you tell them: to flip heads. Of those 128 winners, 64 will flip heads on the next go-round as well. Twice running. Not bad. Thirty-two people will flip heads three times in a row, sixteen will flip heads four times in a row, eight will flip heads five times in a row, four will succeed six times in a row, two will rack up an incredible seven straight successes, and one—one out of 256 in the crowd—will flip heads eight times in a row. What talent! What genius!*
>
> *What nonsense... I'm not saying the stock market is all luck. Nevertheless it is enough of a crap shoot that luck has a great deal more to do with it than any professional money man is going to want to admit.*
>
> *By and large you should manage your own money (via no-load mutual funds). No one is going to care as much about it as you. And no one but you is going to manage it for free.*[44]

If you are going to do your own investing, the next obvious question is, what should you invest your money in? There are a mind-boggling number of choices, but you don't have to be a genius to be a successful investor–many (or most) investments aren't worth taking the time to learn about anyway. So, we'll limit our discussion to the most commonly selected financial

---

[44] Tobias, p166

instruments among investors: bonds, stocks, and mutual funds. (If you're really interested in fancy investment terms like calls, puts, collars, and betas, take a financial markets or investments class, but these are not necessary to earn a good return on your investments.)

7.3. Bonds

A bond is an IOU. It is simply a debt instrument–by purchasing a bond, you are loaning your money to the government or the company that issued the bond and, in return, they are promising to pay you back the amount you loaned them (called the principal) plus interest payments for the opportunity to use your money. For example, suppose you buy a bond from company XYZ for $1,000 and the bond matures in a year and pays 5% interest. That would mean you give the company $1,000 today, and one year from now the company would pay you $1,050. That's the idea behind a bond–it's a lot like purchasing a CD at a bank.[45]

Bonds are issued by the federal government (Treasury bonds), by cities (municipal bonds), and by companies (corporate bonds). The bonds differ in details, like where you buy them, how interest payments are made, and their tax status, but they are all just debt instruments. There are formulas for computing the value of a bond based on its principal (**par value** or face value), **coupon rate** (interest), **maturity** (years until it pays back the principal), and other factors (see Appendix E). The basic result: If the coupon rate is less than the inflation rate, the bond sells at a **discount** (less than par value). If the coupon rate is more than the inflation rate, the bond sells at a **premium** (more than par value). The longer the term to maturity, the greater the discount or premium. Finally, as maturity approaches, all bonds will approach their par value because the coupon and inflation rates no longer matter when there are no more payments.

---

[45] The bond issuer only receives money when the bond is issued (i.e., sold the first time). Bonds are often traded in secondary markets. Any gains or losses in these transactions occur to the bond holder, not the issuer, who continues to pay interest to the bond's new owner.

Treasury Bills, Notes, Bonds, etc. The federal government issues a lot of bonds. Why? Because our federal government routinely spends more money than it collects in taxes. According to the 2017 *Economic Report of the President*, the federal government has run an average budget deficit of 3.2 percent of GDP for the last 40 years.[46] In fact, the federal government has only run a surplus for four years since 1970[47]... that's almost 50 years of living beyond its means. Don't try that with your personal finances!

The last full year of data (2015) shows a total debt of $18.1 trillion owed by the federal government. That number is expected to grow to $20.1 trillion by September 2017.[48] To put that number into perspective, the government's receipts for 2017 are estimated to be $3.6 trillion. That means the federal government owes 558% of what it "earns" in a given year. Let's put that in context using the median income of a U.S. household, $56,000.[49] The equivalent debt would be $312,000, or the equivalent of a very large mortgage. Except in this case, there is no physical asset to back up the debt. The federal debt is not going away anytime soon.

Since the federal government spends more money than it collects in taxes, it has to borrow enough money to cover the deficit each year. To do this, the U.S. Treasury issues bonds called Treasury Bills, Treasury Notes, and Treasury Bonds, depending on the length of time before the security matures. The good news is that Treasury bonds have essentially no risk of default. They are backed by the full credit of the U.S. government, so the only way you will lose your principal is if the U.S. government collapses financially. Another nice feature of Treasury bonds is that any interest you earn on these investments is not taxable by state and local governments (but you still have to pay federal income tax on the interest you earn on them). The bad thing about Treasury Bonds, Notes, and Bills is that they don't generally pay very much interest. So, if you are looking for significant long-term growth, these are

---

[46] p28
[47] 2017 *Economic Report of the President*, p584
[48] 2017 *Economic Report of the President*, p584
[49] Census Bureau p6

probably not very good choices for you–but we'll talk a lot more about that issue later. For now, think of Treasury Bills, Notes, and Bonds as investments that are as safe as any bank deposit, with some possibility of earning a slightly higher return than you'd earn in a bank account or CD.

You can find all the information you'd like about buying and selling Treasury bonds, and you can even open your own account to purchase these bonds, at the Treasury's website: www.treasurydirect.gov. Here is a brief description of each type of security offered:

Treasury Bills are short-term securities with maturity dates measured in weeks (4 to 52). T-Bills come in $1,000 denominations, but you can buy partial bonds for $100. They are sold at a discount and are **zero coupon** bonds. That means they make no regular interest payments. The money you earn is the difference between the original price and the par value at maturity.

Treasury Notes are medium-term securities that have maturity dates from 2 to 10 years. They pay a fixed rate of interest semi-annually (every six months). So if you have a $1,000 Treasury note that has a 4% coupon rate, you will get a $20 interest payment every six months until the note reaches maturity. On the note's maturity date, you will be paid your $1,000 principal, plus your final $20 interest payment.

Treasury Bonds are essentially like Treasury notes, except T-Bonds are issued with a term of 30 years until maturity.

EE Savings Bonds are 30-year bonds that operate like T-Bills. That is, you buy the bond at a discount of the face value, and there are no annual interest payments. Your return is not realized until the bond matures and you are paid the face value of the bond. Your effective interest rate is determined by the amount of the discount when you purchase the bond.

I Savings Bonds are similar to T-Bonds except the interest paid is a combination of the coupon rate and the inflation rate. They are intended to reduce the inflation risk by allowing the bond's return to adjust twice a year.

Treasury Inflation-Protected Securities (TIPS) also reduce inflation risk, but rather than adjust the interest paid, they adjust the principal paid at maturity. They can be purchased with maturities of 5, 10, and 30 years and pay interest every six months at a fixed rate.

Corporate Bonds. Companies also issue bonds. If a corporation is interested in building a new factory or expanding its operations with a new overseas location, it may choose to issue bonds as a way to raise the money to make these investments. Some corporate bonds can be very safe in terms of the risk of default, while others can involve substantial financial risk. Standard & Poor's (www.standardandpoors.com) is a company that evaluates and issues credit ratings on corporate bonds. Standard and Poor's issues credit ratings from AAA (the best) to C (likely to default). As you might expect, corporate bonds with good ratings (AAA, AA, A, and BBB) pay lower interest rates than corporate bonds with weak ratings (BB, B, CCC, CC, and C). The highest rated bonds (AAA) default on their payments less than 1% of the time, but junk bonds (rated CCC or worse) historically default on their payments less than three years after being issued.[50] It's true that junk bonds often offer very high interest rates, but if you purchase one, you are taking a big risk that you may lose your entire investment.

Another consideration with deciding whether to invest in a corporate bond is its **liquidity**. Unlike Treasury securities, there is a much smaller secondary market for corporate bonds. If you want to sell it before it reaches maturity, you may have to pay a substantial commission or accept a deeply discounted price to unload it. Therefore, we generally agree with the advice of Andrew Tobias:

---

[50] Opdyke, pp106-107

Don't buy them. The safest ones, sometimes called investment grade bonds, pay only a bit more than Treasury securities but are subject to state and local taxes... You can find corporate bonds that pay much higher interest than Treasuries. The riskier the bond, the higher the interest you stand to earn. But ordinarily, if you believe in the issuing company, you might as well buy its stock and really profit from its success.[51]

Municipal Bonds. Cities borrow money when they want to start a major construction project and don't have enough tax revenue to pay for it. Municipal bonds are backed by the city government. Technically, they may not be as "safe" from default as U.S. Treasury securities, but it is extremely rare for municipalities to default on bond payments. Between 1986 and 2005, only 0.26% of municipal bonds defaulted on payments, and no municipal bond with a Standard & Poor's credit rating of AAA or AA defaulted.[52] If you purchase a municipal bond issued by your state of residence, the interest payments on the bond are usually exempt from local, state, and federal income taxes. Since municipal bonds are tax exempt, they often pay lower interest rates than other similarly-rated bonds. Nevertheless, the tax-exempt status of municipal bonds makes them appealing to some investors in very high income tax brackets. If you are in a low income tax bracket or are a resident of a state that does not have a state income tax, municipal bonds are unlikely to be a good investment option for you.

One final consideration when purchasing a bond is whether or not it is **callable**. A callable bond is issued with a caveat that if the market interest rate falls far enough, the issuer can force you to redeem the bond early (so you get your principal back, but you do not get the future interest payments). Back in the late 1970s and early 1980s, inflation in the U.S. was running about 10% to 12% per year. During that period, corporations often paid 15% interest, or more, on their bonds. But by 1985, the Federal Reserve had implemented a tight monetary policy and inflation had dropped back to less than 3%. If someone

---

[51] Tobias, p89
[52] Opdyke, pp109-110

purchased a 10 year bond paying 15% nominal interest in 1981, they would have been earning a 12% real rate of return on the bond by 1985. The company that issued the bond would not want to pay 15% interest every year if they could borrow money in 1985 at a much lower interest rate. To avoid that situation, many corporations (and municipalities) only issue callable bonds. Therefore, by 1985, the corporation would simply inform its bond holders that it was calling the bonds and force the bond holders to redeem them early. Even though the bond holders thought they were going to collect 15% interest for the next ten years, they only collected 4 or 5 years of interest because the company called the bond. Therefore, callable bonds often produce much smaller yields (returns) when interest rates are falling than bonds that cannot be called.

The _real_ risk to buying bonds. Bonds can be a sensible part of anyone's portfolio, particularly as people get closer to retirement. Inflation-protected Treasury securities can give an individual some peace of mind that he or she won't suffer a catastrophic loss if there is a major downturn in the stock market or a period of high inflation. However, bonds have historically failed to offer investors the kind of _real_ returns (after adjusting for inflation) needed to build significant wealth. Bonds can be useful for _protecting_ your wealth from loss, but they are poor investment vehicles for building wealth.

A well-known rule of thumb on interest compounding is the **"Rule of 72."** The rule says you can determine roughly how long it will take to double your money by dividing 72 by the percentage returned on an investment. For example, a bond that pays 3% interest will take about 24 years of compounding for the bond to double in value ($72 \div 3 = 24$). But remember, the interest payment on bonds is a nominal interest rate. Even though a 3% nominal investment value doubles in 24 years, it is not really worth twice as much if the dollar's value has been eroded by inflation.

Let's calculate the inflation rate in the U.S. over the last ten years. According to the Federal Reserve Bank of Minneapolis, the CPI-U in 2007 was at 207.3 (with 1982-84 as a base).[53] The

---

[53] CPI-U is the Consumer Price Index for all Urban Consumers.

CPI-U in 2016 was at 239.5. This represents a total growth of $(239.5 - 207.3)/207.3 = 15.5\%$ in 10 years. The annual inflation rate during this period is found by $(1 + r_i)^{10} = 1.155$.[54] Solving for r_i gives an average annual inflation rate of 1.45%. That means the previously discussed 3% bond has a real rate of return of just $3 - 1.45 = 1.55\%$. It will take $72 \div 1.55 = 46.5$ years to double the real value of the investment. That's why bonds aren't very good at building wealth. They just barely keep up with inflation, so your wealth accumulation does not move forward very quickly; it's more like marching in place.

Although the example and numbers we used above are based on recent figures from the last ten years, they aren't far from historical averages in the bond market. Dr. Aswath Damodaran from the Stern School of Business at New York University tracks annual returns for 3-month Treasury Bills, 10-year Treasury Notes, and the S&P 500 index (a representation of the average market return). Based on his data and the CPI-U numbers from the Minneapolis Fed, over the period from 1927 to 2016, the average real return on relatively "riskless" securities (T-Bills) was just 0.3%. That's the real problem with investing too much of your portfolio in bonds; the real rate of return may be so low over the long run that you will be unable to build any significant real wealth before retirement. In contrast, over that same period of time, the stock market outpaced inflation by a much wider margin: 6.4%. At that rate, you're doubling your wealth every $72 \div 6.4 = 11$ years.

If it's hard to grasp how big a difference that makes, let's look at a hypothetical example using real data. Suppose someone was born in 1995 and their generous grandparents made a $1,000 gift investment in either an S&P 500 fund, treasury bills, or treasury notes. The table below shows the normal and real effective annual returns for these investments over the period 1995 to 2016. It also shows the value of the original $1,000 investment in 2016 in both nominal and real dollars. As you can see, the investment in T-Bills only grew by $15 after accounting for inflation. The T-Notes did better, but the stock market return doubled that and more than tripled the original investment over the 21-year period.

---

[54] The math of interest compounding is shown in Appendix E.

Investment Type	Effective Annual Return		Value of Investment	
	Nominal	Real	Nominal	Real
S&P 500	8.3%	6.0%	$5,313.62	$3,373.65
T-Bills	2.3%	0.1%	$1,596.60	$1,015.28
T-Notes	5.1%	3.0%	$2,870.03	$1,858.27

Bonds can give you a feeling of security, but they are unlikely to provide large enough returns to grow your account enough for a comfortable retirement. To do that, you probably need to have a substantial percentage of your account invested in the stock market, to which we turn next.

7.4. Stocks

Although bonds do have some risk, you are technically buying a legal contract that entitles you to money in the future. In contrast, when you buy stock, you are actually buying a portion of the company, and you have no guarantee of future income. That said, there are two ways to make a return on the purchase of stock. First, some stocks pay **dividends**. That means the company shares a portion of its profits with the stockholders. Dividends are short-term earnings that are taxed as regular income for the stockholders (after the company already paid corporate taxes on the money, so it is actually taxed twice). The second way to make money on a stock is through **capital gains** that result from the change in the price of the stock. These gains (or losses) are only realized when you sell the stock, so the tax is deferred. Also, if the stock is held for more than a year, the gains are taxed at the capital gains rate that is usually lower than the rate for regular income.

In addition to potential monetary gains, purchasing a stock gives you a small piece of ownership in a company, which is why stocks are also known as **equities**. Ownership gives you one vote in the company's decisions for each share of stock you own. As a stockholder, you periodically receive correspondence from the company asking for your vote on issues before the board of directors. Most of the time, individual investors own such a small share in the company that they don't wield much voting power, but you can still cast your vote. If you own more than 50% of the stock shares of a company, you control more than 50% of the votes on deciding the company's direction–then you can make yourself the CEO!

Increases and decreases in stock prices do not always occur simultaneously with increases and decreases in company profits. Why is that? Because *stock prices reflect investor expectations about the company's future profitability.* Let's look at an example.

Example #1: Amazon.com. Surely you have heard of Amazon. You have probably purchased books or movies online from Amazon.com. It started out as an online book seller in the mid-1990s, and today it sells everything imaginable. Let's take a look at Amazon's revenues and its net income (profits or losses) from 1997 to 2006, as shown in the table below.[55]

Year	Revenue ($M)	Net Income ($M)
1997	148	−28
1998	610	−125
1999	1,640	−720
2000	2,762	−1,411
2001	3,122	−567
2002	3,933	−149
2003	5,264	35
2004	6,921	588
2005	8,490	359
2006	10,711	190

There are several amazing things about the figures above. The first thing that stands out is how gigantic Amazon is as a retailer. In 2006, Amazon had almost $11B in revenues (yes, that's a "B" as in billion... and it grew to $135B in 2016). The second thing that stands out is how few profits they generated

---

[55] Data from Morningstar.com, an online investment research service.

as a percent of their sales. In 2006, the company earned just $190M in profit on almost $11B in sales; that's just 1.8% profit on revenues. Moreover, Amazon did not even earn a positive annual profit until 2003, when the company had over $5 billion in revenue. Prior to 2003, the company lost money every year, losing a total of about $3B. That's a lot of money to lose in a half-dozen years!

When Amazon had its initial public offering (IPO) in May 1997, the company's investment bankers set the initial stock price at $18 per share.[56] On the day the stock went public, the price went from $18 to $30, then settled back to a closing price of $23.50.[57] That's fairly remarkable since the company *lost money every year* prior to the IPO. If the company had a long history of losing money, how can we possibly explain the sale of 3 million shares of stock at $23 in the first day of public trading? The answer, of course, is that even though the company was not yet profitable, investors clearly expected the company was going to become very profitable in the future. As we pointed out earlier, a stock's price reflects not only the company's current profitability, but also *investor expectations about the company's future profitability.*

In hind-sight, these investors made a great decision. As this sentence is written (22 Feb 2017), Amazon's stock price is $856.33. Not only that, but the stock split several times since the IPO.[58] Someone who bought a share for $23.50 during the IPO now holds 12 shares, each worth $856.33 for a total value of $10,275.96. That is the equivalent of a 36% annualized return. That is some good investing!

Did these investors make a great educated decision or simply get lucky? How do you decide if a stock will be a good investment? Let's look at how to read a stock quote. An online

---

[56] Kawamoto

[57] Kawamoto

[58] A stock split increases the number of shares of stock without issuing new shares. It is a way to reward stockholders. While nothing about the company (or it's expected future profits) changes, the split results in a lower price per share, making the stock *seem* more affordable. This tends to encourage new investors which the company hopes increases the stock price more than it would have without the split.

search for AMZN will generate a gazillion hits–the first of which will probably be financial websites. Most any of them will do: Yahoo finance, Google finance, Morningstar, Market Watch, Money Central, etc. We'll randomly pick Yahoo. Below is the summary from July 25, 2007.

Amazon.com, Inc. (NasdaqGS: AMZN)

Last Trade:	86.17	**Day's Range:**	83.65-88.80
Trade Time:	11:05AM ET	**52wk Range**	29.90-75.35
Change:	↑16.92 (24.43%)	**Volume:**	37,048,121
Prev Close:	69.25	**Avg Vol (3m):**	12,561,800
Open:	84.17	**Market Cap:**	35.30B
Bid:	86.17 x 300	**P/E:**	145.61
Ask:	86.18 x 200	**EPS:**	0.59
1yTarget Est:	63.53	**Div & Yield:**	N/A (N/A)

This table tells us that on the most recent trade of AMZN that morning, the stock sold for $86.17 (**Last Trade**). That trade occurred at 11:05 AM eastern time (**Trade Time**). Note that there is often a small time lag between the real-time trading on the market and the information posted on these websites. We'll talk more about timing later.

The day prior, Amazon stock closed at $69.25 (**Prev Close**), which means the stock price rose $16.92 or 24.4% (**Change**) from the previous close to the last trade. That is a huge swing in price in less than a day. The price range that the stock has traded at over the past year is $29.90 to $75.35 (**52wk Range**), so if the stock continues trading in the high 80s on this day, it will set a new record high for the year. With 37 million shares of the stock trading (**Volume**), the stock is very busy today compared to the average volume over the last three months of only 12 million shares (**Avg Vol (3m)**).

Elsewhere on Yahoo's financial website for AMZN, we find that Amazon has about 410 million shares of stock outstanding. If we multiply the number of shares of stock times the price per share (410M x $86) we get the size of the company's **market capitalization** which, in this case, is $35.3B (**Market Cap**). This is a simple estimate of the value or worth of a company (without actually accounting for physical assets, reputation, products, etc.)

Amazon does not pay a dividend, so the quote has N/A for **Div & Yield**. The last two figures we'll discuss are Amazon's price-to-earnings ratio (**P/E**) and its earnings per share (**EPS**). These are both key numbers for investors.

Every publicly traded company is required to publish certain information with the Securities and Exchange Commission (SEC). This includes an income statement, a cash flow statement, and a balance sheet. We are not going to get into the details of these reports, but they can usually be accessed from financial websites or directly from the SEC. According to Amazon's filings, the company made approximately $250M in net income (profit) in its fiscal year 2007.[59] So a little simple math tells us that if the company earned $250M and it has 410M shares of stock, the earnings per share of stock is roughly $250M ÷ 410M = 60 cents per share, which corresponds with the EPS 0.59 reported above. If Amazon's EPS is $0.60 and the price of one share of stock is selling for $86, then the Price to Earnings ratio (P/E) is 86 ÷ 0.60 = 143. (Above, the actual P/E ratio is 145.6.)

Now that you know how the numbers are calculated, what do they mean? Let's put this into perspective by comparing Amazon's stock with something more mundane, such as a bank CD. In July 2007, you could put your money into a CD at the local bank and earn 4% interest, guaranteed (FDIC insured).[60] Suppose you put $86 into one of these CDs in the bank and withdrew it a year later. You would have gotten $86(1.04) = $89.44 back, which means you would have earned $3.44 interest on your $86 deposit. Your CD's price-to-earnings ratio would be 86 ÷ 3.44 = 25. (This is the inverse of the annual interest rate.) So the guaranteed CD earnings were nearly six times greater than the earnings on Amazon stock. That's a huge difference. Why would anyone buy Amazon with a P/E

---

[59] SEC Form 8-K, Exhibit 99.1 p5
[60] Mazzucco. Technically, 4% was the 5-year rate, but we used the number to simplify the math.

ratio of 145, when they can essentially get a P/E ratio of 25 guaranteed at the bank?[61] Good question!

Even relative to the stock market, Amazon's P/E of 145 is astronomical. According to research published by the Kansas City Federal Reserve, the average P/E ratio for U.S. stocks for the 127-year period from 1872 to 1998 was just 14.[62] A P/E ratio of 14 roughly corresponds to an annual return rate of a little more than 7%. So, again, why would anyone buy a stock with a P/E ratio of 145, when the historical average P/E of U.S. stocks is one-tenth that amount?

At a stock price of $86, in order to drive Amazon's P/E ratio down to 25 over the next year, the company would have to earn an annual net income of $3.44 per share, and with 410 million shares outstanding, that means the company has to earn an annual income of over $1.4 billion in 2007. Possible–perhaps. Probable–NO WAY!

So, if the stock quote did not make Amazon look like a good investment, why did investors buy Amazon stock in 2007? This leads to the next discussion about the stock market: *expectations* and *speculation*. Let's take a look at the historical fluctuations in the stock price of Amazon for the period we're investigating. The chart below comes from Big Charts, a service of Market Watch.[63]

---

[61] Since P/E ratio is the inverse of the interest rate for the CD (1/0.04 = 25), the implied interest rate for Amazon's P/E ratio of 145 would be 0.7%.
[62] Shen, p24
[63] http://bigcharts.marketwatch.com/

The chart shows huge price fluctuations. Since 1998, the price of Amazon has fluctuated from under $10 to over $110. Relatively speaking, the stock's price fluctuations have been much, much larger than the fluctuations in the company's revenues or profits. It's crazy, but that's the stock market!

Stock prices usually fluctuate much more than the fundamental financial numbers of a company. That's because stock prices reflect investor's **expectations** about the company's future. Expectations involve predicting the future–so stock prices regularly undershoot and overshoot the actual company's performance (particularly because people have a hard time containing their emotions when investing in the stock market). When a company appears to be doing well, investors may exuberantly jump on the bandwagon and buy the stock. But the supply of the stock (number of shares) has not changed, so the increased demand for the stock drives the price up to sometimes dizzying heights. On the other hand, when a company reports actual earnings below the expectations of investors, people may fear the company's future earnings outlook is poor and start selling the stock, thereby driving down the price. While an individual company may experience relatively mild changes in revenue and profits, the company's stock can still endure large price swings.[64]

Another reason stock prices fluctuate is due to **speculation**. Some investors may be buying the stock, not because they want to hold onto it for a long time as the company grows, but simply because they are seeking to make a quick profit from a rapid rise in the stock's price. If an investor bought Amazon six months before the quote above, when it cost just $38, and sold it for $86, the investor would have doubled his or her money in a very short time, even though nothing fundamentally had changed about the company in the previous months. For high-visibility companies with large volumes of trading, we suspect much (perhaps most) of the large price swings in the stock are due to speculation–investors attempting to make a profit on a

---

[64] A great example was Chipotle Mexican Grill (CMG) on Feb 14, 2008. Despite an earnings report that showed increases in revenues (31.5%) and profit margins (8.9%), the company missed it's EPS projection by a penny ($0.53 instead of $0.54). As a result, the stock price dropped 13.9% the day after the report. Baertlein

quick sale, without much regard for the long-term performance of the company. When it comes to the stock market, there's another term that's synonymous with speculation–it's called *gambling*! Using your investment accounts to speculate in the market is not investing, it is gambling, and you will eventually get burned.

Would it make sense for you to withdraw all of your retirement savings, fly to Las Vegas, walk in to a casino, and place the entire amount on "red" or "black" at the roulette table? Of course not! Don't try to speculate with your investments in the stock market either–the odds are about the same, maybe even worse in the stock market because you have to pay commissions every time you place a bet. Also, any gains you make on stocks held less than a year are taxed the same as regular income. However, Vegas thrives because some people do enjoy gambling. (That's called *risk-seeking* behavior.) If you enjoy tracking stocks and making frequent trades, that's OK; but just like going to Vegas, you should only do it with money you can afford to lose, not as part of your investment strategy.

Recall that there are two ways to make money on stocks: dividends and capital gains. Stable companies may not offer the huge returns of successful internet startups, but they are safer and still offer good returns. It's like the tortoise and the hare.

Example #2: NextEra Energy. Unlike Amazon, you probably haven't heard of NextEra Energy. You should do a lot of research before putting money into a company you know nothing about. As before, financial websites have lots of free information available. Sticking with Yahoo for consistency, here is a description of NextEra:

NextEra Energy, Inc., through its subsidiaries, generates, transmits, and distributes electric energy in the United States and Canada. The company generates electricity from gas, oil, solar, coal, petroleum coke, nuclear, and wind sources. As of December 31, 2015, it served approximately 9.5 million people through approximately 4.8 million customer accounts in the east and lower west coasts of Florida. The company had approximately 46,400 megawatts

*of generating capacity. It also leases fiber-optic network
capacity and dark fiber to telephone, wireless, and Internet
companies. The company was formerly known as FPL
Group, Inc. and changed its name to NextEra Energy, Inc.
in 2010. NextEra Energy, Inc. was founded in 1984 and is
headquartered in Juno Beach, Florida.* [65]

Below is the stock quote from 10:07AM Eastern on Feb 23,
2017.

NextEra Energy, Inc. (NYSE: NEE)

Last Trade:	128.94	**Day's Range:**	128.61-129.26
Trade Time:	10:07AM ET	**52wk Range**	109.34-131.98
Change:	↑0.50 (0.39%)	**Volume:**	136,509
Prev Close:	128.44	**Avg Vol (3m):**	1,956,903
Open:	128.75	**Market Cap:**	60.39B
Bid:		**P/E:**	20.68
Ask:		**EPS:**	6.25
1yTarget Est:	126.73	**Div & Yield:**	3.93 (3.06%)

This company's P/E is more in line with the historic average of
the market. It equates to about a $1/20 = 5\%$ return. That is a
decent, if not spectacular, return for an investment. However,
note that NEE pays dividends. If the company continues to pay
dividends at $3.93 per share, you will earn a $$3.93/$128.94 =$
3.06% return on your investment from the dividend. When you
add that to the expected return on the stock price, it seems like
a much more reasonable investment.

We don't mean to imply that a company that pays dividends is
automatically a better investment. By paying dividends, the
company has less profit to reinvest and grow the company.
That means, the stock price will likely grow at a lower rate than
a company that does not pay dividends. Also, remember that
dividends are taxed as regular income. So, don't simply look for
stocks paying large dividends, but rather try to select stocks
that will return the highest profit overall (which includes
dividends and stock price) after taxes.

---

[65] http://finance.yahoo.com/quote/NEE/profile?p=NEE

So, how do you find a good stock to purchase? The best advice we have is to look for value–which means well-managed companies, that are undervalued by investors. That sounds easy, but it's not. First, you don't have a crystal ball to see the future, and everything about a stock is either historical data or expectations about the future. Also, everyone else is looking for the same thing. Just about any fancy financial calculations you use to determine that a company is undervalued based on its stock price has probably already been done by lots of other people who are also looking to identify these good stock buys. When everyone chases the same undervalued stock, its price will rise, making it no longer undervalued.

The **efficient market hypothesis** suggests that new information about a company's performance gets incorporated into the company's stock price so quickly that investors cannot, on average, do better than just holding a random sampling of stocks. In his now-famous paper on efficient capital markets, Eugene Fama concluded, *"the theory of efficient markets is concerned with whether prices at any point in time 'fully reflect' available information... In short, the evidence in support of the efficient markets model is extensive."*[66] Look at the NextEra quote again. You've probably never heard of them, but nearly 2 million shares are traded on the average day. Consider the average daily volume for well-known companies: 3.6M for Amazon, 24.2M for Microsoft, 29.3M for Apple, 35.4M for Ford. Of course, some of these trades could be based only on emotion, but there surely are many investors in the market that pay attention to the companies' news releases, carefully read the companies' financial and business reports, and do their homework on the companies very carefully before making a trade. *These people are your real competition!* So, in truth, it is extremely difficult for anyone to consistently pick stocks that perform better than average.

In a review of over 40 years of published research on stock market performance, Princeton economics professor Burton Malkiel found "a remarkably large body of evidence suggests that professional investment managers are not able to outperform index funds that buy and hold the broad stock

---

[66] Fama pp413, 416

market portfolio."[67] Reviewing the performance of professional portfolio managers over 10-, 15-, and 20-year periods, Malkiel found that "the median large-capitalization professionally managed equity fund has underperformed the S&P 500 index by almost 2 percentage points... moreover, those funds that produce excess returns in one period are not likely to do so in the next. There is no dependable persistence in performance."[68] Therefore, if the average full-time stock market professional cannot beat the market with his stock picks, what do you think the probability is that the average investor can do it as a hobby?

There's another problem with buying individual stocks on your own. Unless you have a big pile of money, it's hard to buy enough different stocks to really diversify your portfolio. **Diversification** means buying stocks in different companies that engage in a lot of different types of businesses. For example, a well-diversified portfolio would contain stocks in technology companies, energy companies, financial companies, utilities, transportation, pharmaceutical companies, and other sectors of the economy. Portfolio diversification reduces your risk of being wiped out by one or two bad stock picks. Mathematically, investors measure risk by looking at the **variance** of the returns. Diversification looks at the **covariance**, which is based on how closely two different investment returns are correlated. Investments that are perfectly negatively correlated would be ideal for diversification, but ideal rarely happens in reality. On the plus side, as long as the investments are not perfectly positively correlated, holding both will reduce the portfolio risk compared to a portfolio with only one of the investments.

Big piles of cash also making trading easier. Go back to the Amazon quote. Notice the bid and ask prices were for lots of 200 and 300 shares. Brokers typically make trades in **even lots** (i.e., multiples of 100 shares). If you place an order (buy or sell) for less than 100 shares, a broker will wait until there are other orders to make an even lot. That means the price you get will not be the same as what you think it is when you place the

---

[67] Malkiel, p77
[68] Malkiel, p78

purchase. (This timing is especially important if you're gambling with day trading.)

So after all that learning about stocks, stock quotes, and basic stock valuation using P/E ratios, EPS, and dividend yields, we ruined things by telling you the stock market is very efficient, so people generally are unable to consistently pick stocks that do better than just a random selection of stocks. On top of that, you need lots of cash to diversity your portfolio and reduce your risk of a potentially catastrophic loss. We've probably made it sound really, really difficult to be a successful stock market investor. Don't fret. It's actually not hard at all to invest wisely in the stock market. Just buy shares in a broadly diversified, no-load mutual fund, and you won't have to worry about all of the details above.

7.5. Mutual Funds

A mutual fund allows small investors to pool their money and buy a collection of many stocks, bonds, and other investments so average folks with just a little money can own a well-diversified portfolio and have professional management. Another benefit is that most mutual funds have no transaction fees, unlike stocks, which incur a broker fee for each transaction. This allows monthly dollar-cost averaging (explained below).

There are thousands of mutual funds you can invest in; some are diversified across the entire stock market, and some are focused on bonds or on individual sectors within the market. You can buy mutual funds from discount brokers online, many of which are sold with no load and no transaction fees.[69] For example, Charles Schwab offers access through their website to more than 2,000 no-load mutual funds with no transaction fees. Scottrade offers access to over 1,000 no-load mutual funds with no transaction fees. You can also buy mutual funds directly through the fund company. For example, Vanguard sells some terrific mutual funds, such as their S&P 500 index

---

[69] A load is basically a sales charge on a mutual fund. There are thousands of no-load mutual funds which perform just as well (or better) than funds with these extra charges. Don't buy a loaded fund.

fund (VFINX), which has an expense ratio of just 0.16% and tracks the S&P 500 very closely.[70] The choices are staggering. Fortunately, there are tools available online that can help you narrow down your selection.

One of the most useful websites is Morningstar.com, which provides independent investment research. The site has a free side (after registration) and you can access the premium side for free for 14 days. Morningstar's website provides great information about almost any fund. Morningstar is also famous for its star-rating system. Morningstar's stars were developed to provide a quick snapshot of how each fund has performed relative to its peers (e.g., domestic stock funds, international stock funds, etc.) with respect to the mutual fund's risk-adjusted return, "which also accounts for the effects of all sales charges, loads, and redemption fees."[71] According to Morningstar, "The rating accounts for all variations in a fund's monthly performance, with more emphasis on downward variations. It rewards consistent performance and reduces the possibility of strong short-term performance masking the inherent risk of a fund."[72] The funds with returns (after expenses) and price stability in the top 10% relative to their peers are given 5 stars. The next 22.5% of funds receive 4 stars, the middle 35% of funds receive 3 stars, the next 22.5% earn 2 stars, and the bottom 10% are given just 1 star.[73]

However, before you just start buying 5-star rated funds, it's important to keep in mind that the stars are based on the funds' past performance. Just because a mutual fund performed well last year is no guarantee it will continue to perform well in the future. Lots of things can change (like a turnover in the fund's management), which might cause a 5-star rated fund to perform poorly. In fact, economics research suggests "there is no dependable persistence in performance" of mutual funds.[74] So

---

[70] Tobias, p234; We used Vanguard as an example thanks to Mr. Jerry Bruni, the owner of a highly successful investment management firm in Colorado Springs. (He was also Rich Fullerton's economics teacher and academic advisor at USAFA.)
[71] "The Morningstar Rating for Funds," p2
[72] "The Morningstar Rating for Funds," p2
[73] "The Morningstar Rating for Funds," p2
[74] Malkiel, p78

don't use Morningstar's star-rating system alone as your sole source for a buy recommendation, but do explore the valuable information at Morningstar's website.

Now, let's take a look at a few different types of mutual funds. In particular, there are four mutual fund categories we will review because these are terms you are certain to run into as you begin exploring investments: open-end funds, closed-end funds, money-market funds, and life cycle funds.

Open-End Mutual Funds. If a fund is open-ended, this means there is no limit to the number of shares the fund is able to sell. For an open-end fund, the share price is just the fund's assets divided by its number of shares. Jeff Opdyke offers the following description of how open-end funds operate:

> If a [open-end] fund has $10 million in assets and it has issued one million shares, then each share is priced at $10... If you come along and buy $1,000 of the fund, then it issues you 100 shares. The result: The fund has assets of $10,001,000 and 1,000,100 shares outstanding, which still equals $10 per share. Open-end mutual funds do not trade on any stock exchange. Instead, they're sold and redeemed by the mutual fund company itself. Unlike stocks, where prices change through the day, open-end funds price their shares just once a day, after the market closes when the fund calculates the cumulative value of all its investments.[75]

Closed-End Mutual Funds. A closed-end mutual fund has a specific, limited number of shares set on the day the fund begins trading; from that point on, the mutual fund's shares are traded just like shares of a regular company. Suppose a closed-end fund begins with one million shares trading at $10 per share. Then, for the life of the fund, it will always have just 10 million shares, unless the shareholders vote to change the number of shares (like a company would do with a stock split). If the closed-end fund's initial stock purchases are terrific and the fund's net asset value (NAV) increases to $11 million, then with just 10 million shares of the fund on the market, the

---

[75] Opdyke, p115

underlying value of each share (based on the fund's assets) would be $11 per share. But that is not necessarily the price shares of the fund will trade at! Since this is a closed-end fund, its share price is determined by supply and demand, just like a regular stock. These funds' shares trade on exchanges, just like stocks, and their share prices fluctuate up and down throughout the day as investors buy and sell shares. So even though a closed-end fund's NAV may be $11 per share, the actual market price of the share could be higher or lower, depending on investor demand. If the fund's shares are trading above NAV, it is trading at a premium. (It's hard to imagine why a person would pay a premium for a closed-end fund.) If the fund's share price is trading below NAV, the fund is said to be trading at a discount. If you go to Morningstar's website, you can select closed-end funds and sort their list based on the funds selling at the largest discounts. A closed-end fund might be a good investment if you can buy its shares at a discount, but be cautious. One reason closed-end funds frequently trade at a discount is because they often have high management and administrative fees.

Money Market Mutual Funds. If you invest your money with a discount broker, you will often have some money in the account that is not tied up in any particular stock or mutual fund. Or you may sell a mutual fund and decide not to reinvest the money you gained from the sale until a later date. When that happens, it would be nice to have a way to earn a modest amount of interest on the "cash" that you have sitting in your account. That's what money market mutual funds are used for. Money market mutual funds are open-end funds that invest in short term, low-risk securities. Don't confuse a money market mutual fund with the "money market account" that you open in a bank, as we discussed earlier. Money market accounts at banks are FDIC insured. Money market mutual funds are not. It is possible to lose money in a money market mutual fund, but it's unlikely. These funds are simply a convenient place to stash your cash and earn a little interest until you're ready to invest in a longer term instrument with greater earnings potential. In most cases, your discount broker will automatically "sweep" any excess cash in your account into a money market fund, so it will be as accessible to you as cash while still earning a small return. Of course, because the return is small, this is not the place to permanently invest your money. It is important to keep the money in your account working for you by keeping it invested.

Life Cycle Funds. A life cycle fund is really just a mutual fund that invests in a mix of stocks and bonds (or even other mutual funds), targeted for a particular retirement date. When you are young and have a long time to invest before retirement, the stock market is generally your best investment because over long time horizons, the stock market has historically outperformed bonds by a wide margin. However, the stock market can and does drop periodically and, on rare occasions, has been known to crash. For example, after the financial crisis of 2008, the S&P 500 lost 37% of its value. That was one of the largest stock collapses on record. Yet, 10 years later, the S&P has nearly tripled in value, and the 10-year annualized return exceeds 7%. Your patience with the market would have paid off handsomely, even if you invested in the market just prior to the 2008 crash. The idea behind life cycle funds is that the funds' assets are allocated with a target retirement date in mind. When a life cycle fund is decades away from the targeted retirement date, the fund's assets are invested heavily in stocks. As the fund gets closer to the selected retirement year, the fund will progressively reallocate its portfolio towards a larger percentage of bonds to protect investors against major loss if there is a stock market crash just before they retire.

Regardless of the type of mutual fund, they all operate essentially the same, from an investor's perspective. Your return is based on the rise and fall of the underlying value of the investments the fund holds (except for closed-end funds). For all of them, the value also changes based on fees charged by the mutual fund company. These fees could include loads (or transaction fees) and management fees.

A **load** just refers to paying a fee when you buy or sell shares in the fund. Either way, it's a bad deal. Loaded mutual funds are often pitched by salespersons or brokers as good investments because (they claim) the load is used to pay for expert, professional management of the mutual fund. _Don't believe it!_ Most likely, the load just pays for sales commissions to the people who are aggressively pushing you to buy the fund. Just about every empirical study we've seen comparing the actual performance of load versus no-load mutual funds finds that no-load funds perform just as well (often better) than loaded funds. For example, a large study of the performance of 8,100 different mutual funds from 1983 to 1997 concluded, "*In general, given a risk-adjusted basis by investment category, no-load funds performed better than load funds.*"[76] Don't waste your money on a loaded fund.

In addition to ensuring there is no load, check out a fund's **management and administrative fees**. Many actively managed mutual funds have fees exceeding 2%. That is, the mutual fund company will charge you 2% of your account value once a year to cover its expenses. Andrew Tobias offers good advice when he says, "You have to have a very good reason to go with a fund that charges you more than 1% a year for its management and administration."[77] Realize that means the fund must outperform the market by more than the fee in order for you to actually be better off than just investing in the market. Worse, your taxes will be higher with a mutual fund that has a lot of active trading, generating short-term capital gains that are taxed as normal income. This is frequently an unpleasant surprise to new investors when tax time comes. Funds do not withhold taxes, so investors can have large out-of-pocket expenses when they file their taxes. So how do you keep up with the market at minimum cost? Index funds.

An **index fund** seeks to mimic the returns of an established market index. The benefit of an index fund is very low fees, well below 1%. As an example, the Vanguard S&P 500 index fund (VFINX) has annual expenses of only 0.16%. According to Morningstar, over the last 15 years, VFINX has been within 0.12% of the actual S&P 500 index. That means you can get a return after expenses within 0.3% of the S&P 500. That would likely put you ahead of the average investor. According to research, of 158 mutual funds that survived from 1970-2001, more than half of the funds (86) averaged returns that were at least 1% below the S&P 500.[78] Since most funds are unable to

---

[76] Kuhle & Pope, p7
[77] Tobias, p232
[78] Malkiel, p80

even match the S&P 500 in their performance, the Vanguard 500 Index fund (and other similar index funds with low annual expenses) would appear to be very sound investments.

If you don't want to mimic the S&P 500 index, there are other indices you can follow as well (see Appendix D). The Russell 2000 index is a collection of small U.S. companies with an average market capitalization of $2.1B (okay, not exactly tiny companies, but smaller than the S&P 500).[79] Many investors prefer investing in small stocks because during some periods, small stocks have earned larger average returns than large stocks. Of course, during other periods, the large stocks performed better. There are also indices that track international stocks, like the Nikkei 225, which tracks companies traded on the Japanese stock market. There are even indices that track specific sectors, such as the Pharmaceutical Index, which tracks big U.S. pharmaceutical companies. If you are going to invest in an index fund, however, please bear two points in mind:

1. Invest the largest portion of your funds in a broadly diversified index fund–something that tracks the S&P 500, or the Russell 2000, or the S&P Midcap 400 (for medium sized companies). Specialized indices, like the pharmaceutical index or a technology index, can leave you at some risk if that sector of the economy takes a hit.

2. Make sure your index fund has low annual expenses. That is a primary advantage to investing in an index fund; it's a no-brainer for the fund managers. Index fund managers do not have to think a lot about what to buy – they just buy the stocks listed in the index (the funds are "passively" managed). It's not that hard. Therefore, index fund expenses should be correspondingly low–definitely below 1%, and more on the order of ½ percent or less.

---

[79] Russell 2000 Index Fact Sheet, p1

7.6. Investment Advice

With all those options, investing can definitely seem overwhelming. Before we give you our advice on how best to do it (in our opinion), there are a few more topics to cover regardless of the type of investment you choose.

Opportunity Cost and Goals. We already discussed the opportunity cost of your money. It doesn't make sense to save money at a low return while carrying a balance on a high interest rate credit card. You need to get control of your finances before you can start a consistent investment program. Also, consider your goals and situation in life. If you haven't established your emergency expense account (one to two months' pay), you should not be putting money into a retirement account that you cannot access until much later in life. Also, if you're planning a big purchase (like a car or a house) in the near future, you probably do not want all of your investment money going into retirement accounts. That said, once you've met your short-term goals, it's usually best to take full advantage of your retirement options.

Market Timing. The previous discussion raises the question of when you should invest your money into a mutual fund, stock, bond, or other long-term investment instrument of your choice. Sometimes, investing in the market can be a maddening experience. Both of your authors have experienced bad days in the market. One example: On July 25, 2007, one of us had money sitting in a money market fund earning a paltry amount of interest. As soon as it was invested in the market, the S&P 500 dropped from $1,518$ down to $1,458$–that was a 4% loss in the first two days. Ouch! When those things happen, you want to pull your hair out. You just sit there and think, "If I had only waited two more days before investing, I would be much better off." So the tendency for many people is to try and "time" the market. They'll have money to invest, then sit day after day watching the market and waiting for it to drop–they'll try to buy into the market (or a stock or mutual fund) right after the price falls. Of course, the problem with this strategy is that while you are waiting, the market may just continue to rise and rise, and you will have missed a great opportunity.

Indeed, the evidence suggests that "timing the market" is generally a losing strategy. From one day to the next, it's anyone's guess whether the market is going to rise or fall. If you're trying to time the market, you are just guessing, too! Remember the efficient market hypothesis.... nobody knows for sure if the market is going to rise or fall tomorrow–and you're just as likely to miss a big market rally as you are to avoid a market drop. The stock market tends to move in big spurts, so it is critical to actually be in the market when it makes a move upward. Therefore, the general rule is that ***time in the market is more important than timing the market***.

According to the Schwab Center for Investment Research, between 1997 and 2006, the S&P 500 index grew an average of 8.4% per year.[80] Over that period, if you were out of the market the top 10 days, your average annual return would have been just 3.4%, and if you were out of the market the top 20 days, your average annual return would have been *negative* 0.4%.[81] So it is more important to have your money invested in the market rather than taking a chance on missing the big days while you're trying to time the market. Get in the market for the long term, and don't let short-term turbulence keep you from participating.

Dollar-Cost Averaging. Since it's more important to be in the market, you shouldn't hold back from investing when you have the funds, particularly if you are purchasing an investment, like a mutual fund, that has no transaction costs. If you set money aside each month from your paycheck into your retirement or investment account, you can actually buy the investment cheaper by making regular purchases because of dollar-cost averaging. Here's an example: Suppose you are buying a mutual fund with no transaction costs and you have $300 set aside from your paycheck each month in which to purchase the mutual fund. Let's assume the mutual fund share price is $10 the first month, $20 the second month and $15 the third month. The average price of the mutual fund during these three months is $15. If you saved your money until the third month,

---

[80] Sonders, p11
[81] Sonders, p11

you would have $900 saved up and could purchase 60 shares of the mutual fund at the average price of $15 per share.

Now, instead, suppose you purchased shares of the fund every month. The first month, at $10 per share, you could purchase 30 shares. The second month, at $20 per share, you could purchase 15 shares. The last month, at $15 per share, you could purchase 20 shares. Therefore, if you bought shares when you had the money each month, you would end up with a total of $30 + 15 + 20 = 65$ shares of the mutual fund, so you end up with 5 more shares than if you bought all of the shares at the "average" share price. This is because of dollar-cost averaging.[82]

From month to month, you cannot predict whether the price will go up or down, so there's no advantage to holding your money to try and "time" the market, as discussed in the previous section. However, by purchasing shares on a regular basis, you end up buying more shares than if you bought shares all at once at the average price. Dollar-cost averaging works because, when the share price is low, you automatically buy more shares. Similarly, when the share price is high, you buy fewer shares. Of course, if you are buying an investment with a transaction fee (commission) associated with the purchase, you may be better off delaying your buy until you have a larger sum of money to avoid paying too many commissions. But if you're buying a mutual fund with no load and no transaction fee (and there are many out there), you are generally better off making the purchase as soon as you have funds to buy.

High Risk Investments. Without a doubt, at some point in your life, someone is going to try and lure you into buying some kind of high-risk investment such as futures, stock options, commodities, etc. Don't do it! We're not going to discuss these investments because they are not the way to wisely invest for the long-term. If you want to learn about them, buy an investment book or take a finance course on portfolio management. Then, after you really, really understand all of the details—still don't buy them. If you want to gamble with your

---

[82] If the share price in the last month were the lowest price, that would be the best option, but you never know when the lowest price will occur, so dollar-cost averaging is better in general.

money, you'll probably do better flying to Vegas and putting everything down on "red" for one single spin. At least then you will almost have a 50% chance of winning.

Our Advice. People achieve financial success the same way they achieve success in other endeavors: through discipline and patient practice of their craft. Similarly, increasing your net worth requires disciplined saving and patient investing over a long period of time. But even a large proportion of high wage earners in the United States fail to adequately save for their retirements. The top reason earners from almost every income category give for failing to save more money is that they need to pay bills. The problem is not that we Americans don't make enough money–it's that we don't budget appropriately for the income we earn. Investment advisor P.J. DiNuzzo calls it the **105 percent rule**: "If they're making $100,000, they spend $105,000. If they're making $200,000, they're spending $210,000. They say they'll start making it up next year, and then next year turns into 10, 15, or 20 years down the road and they've wasted a tremendous opportunity to prepare for retirement."[83] Also, many people don't see the benefit of savings. Warner and Pleeter studied the military drawdown program of the early 1990s to estimate personal discount rates. Looking at over 65,000 people who chose to separate from the military and made a choice between an annuity and a lump-sum payment, they estimated the implied discount rates could be as high as 30%.[84] With discount rates that high, no investment would provide a sufficient return to give up present consumption.

In our opinion, your first priority is to get control of your finances by establishing and sticking to a budget. Next, pay off your high-interest credit cards and establish your emergency expense fund. Don't forget to grow that fund as your life situation changes and your monthly expenses grow. With that out of the way, determine your allocation for retirement (tax-deferred) and non-retirement accounts. Unless you have specific purchases in mind, we recommend putting as much into tax-deferred accounts as possible in order to get the best return on your investments. Ideally, if you're saving at least 10%

---

[83] Bruce
[84] p33

of your income, at some point you will reach your maximum allowable contributions for tax-deferred accounts and more of your investments will go into taxable accounts. That's a great situation to be in, but it likely will not happen until your late thirties, or possibly later.

For both retirement and non-retirement accounts, our opinion is that the best investment for the average person is a no-load, open-end index fund with low administrative and management fees. If you're saving for near-term purchases (less than five years), move some money to "safer" income or dividend funds. This approach is not as glamorous as buying individual stocks, but you're likely to be better off in the long run, with a higher after-tax and after-expenses return. If you really want to play the market and you enjoy doing all the investment research, do so as a hobby, not as part of your overall investment strategy. You should only gamble with money you're willing to lose.

Remember, the very first lesson in economics is scarcity. It's a fact that you will never have enough money to buy everything you want in life. So, don't try to have it all right away—get into the habit of saving part of every paycheck and developing a disciplined financial lifestyle. This is easiest if you start that way from the very beginning, before your lifestyle eats up your income.

Finally, although this is an introduction to investing, we don't want to leave you with the impression that life is simply about the accumulation of wealth. Money, by itself, is a pretty poor way to "keep score" in life. If you really want to keep score, count the things that matter: your family and friends, your faith, your service to your fellow man—those are things that really matter, in our opinion, and the things you will be most thankful for at the end of your life. That is why we included a budget line for charity in Chapter 3. It is an important part of our Christian faith, and charitable giving is also an important part of most other religions.[85] Even apart from religious motivation, most of us feel better about ourselves if we give something to those

---

[85] The tithe is a traditional part of Jewish and Christian religions. Charitable giving is one of the five pillars of Islam, and charity is also a key element of other world religions like Buddhism and Hinduism.

who are less fortunate or to a cause we believe in. It is great to accumulate wealth–not for the money, but for the things your wealth may allow you to do: support your family, send your children to college, provide for your retirement, and give to those who are in need so you can help make the world a better place.

Chapter 8. Insurance

8.1. What is Insurance?

We decided to briefly write about insurance because chances are that someday an insurance salesman is going to try and sell you life insurance as "a good investment." It is not. Understanding what insurance is will clarify this point. The topic can get confusing because the Affordable Care Act has politicians and talking heads everywhere confounding the terms healthcare and health insurance. Insurance is about managing risk. A healthcare plan incorporates insurance but also involves pooling customers to increase their market power and enable them to negotiate lower prices (which is actually illegal for suppliers to do, except for suppliers of labor).

How does insurance manage risk? If you think about it, most events in life are random and are associated with different costs or payoffs based on these random events. That's a little bit like gambling. Insurance allows you to control the payoffs of the gamble to eliminate the uncertainty. Let's look at a simple car insurance example.

Suppose there are only two possible events when you own a car. There's a 10% chance of having an accident and a 90% chance of no accident. For simplicity, we'll assume the accident will cost you $5,000. If there's no accident, you do not incur any other costs, so the payoff is $0. If you consider driving your car in this scenario, you're essentially playing the "game" shown to the right. The expected value is a loss of $500.[86] Losing $500 is bad, but in reality,

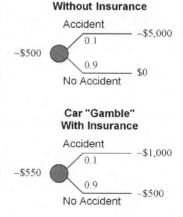

Car "Gamble"
Without Insurance

Accident
0.1 ———— –$5,000
–$500
0.9
———— $0
No Accident

Car "Gamble"
With Insurance

Accident
0.1 ———— –$1,000
–$550
0.9
———— –$500
No Accident

---

[86] $0.1(-\$5,000) + 0.9(\$0) = -\$500$

this could be a catastrophic situation because 10% of the time, you actually lose $5,000.

Now let's suppose you can buy an auto insurance policy with a $500 **premium** (i.e., what you pay for the policy) and a $500 **deductible** (i.e., what you pay when you use the policy).[87] So, no matter what happens, you pay $500, but if you get in an accident, you pay the deductible rather than the full $5,000.[88] The "game" with updated payoffs from the insurance policy is shown on the right. The expected value now is a loss of $550. That may seem worse because you lose more money on average, but it is a less risky scenario. With the insurance, there is no chance of losing $5,000. If you choose to buy this policy, you are willing to lose $50 (in terms of expected value) to avoid the original scenario. We call that $50 a **risk premium**.[89]

This example may seem weird because every state mandates specific types of auto insurance coverage and none of it looks like this. The scenario is admittedly simplified to illustrate the point, but it is exactly how insurance markets started. Commodities markets essentially provide insurance for farmers against uncertain crop prices. A farmer buys a policy from a commodities broker to sell at a guaranteed price (likely lower than the expected crop price). That way, the farmer only worries about crop yield and eliminates the uncertainty about the market price. If there is a boom year and prices drop, the broker takes the loss. On the other hand, if there is a drought or some other event that creates unusually low production, the broker benefits from the higher prices. In either scenario, the farmer receives the same price for his crop.

---

[87] Deductibles are included in insurance policies to avoid **moral hazard** (people taking unnecessary risks). By having to pay a deductible, the consumer still bears part of the risk.

[88] The payoff is −$1,000 because you pay both the premium and the deductible

[89] We are using the language loosely here. Truly calculating a risk premium for a risk-averse person requires the use of the person's utility function, which is more than we care to get into for an introduction to the topic.

8.2. Types of Insurance

There are many types of insurance, and you will run into more and more of them as your financial life gets more complicated. Below we discuss some of the more common types.

Auto Insurance. Auto insurance is required by law, but there are many elective options that can make your premiums much more expensive. Most states require you to have **personal injury protection** (PIP), which pays your medical bills after an accident, and **liability**, to pay other people's expenses should you be at fault in the accident. Insurance companies also offer:

- **Collision** - pays to fix your car when an accident is your own fault
- **Comprehensive** - pays for theft or damage caused by things other than collisions (vandalism, hail, etc.)
- **Uninsured Motorist** - covers costs if the person liable for an accident does not have insurance or is under-insured
- **Rental car reimbursement** - pays for a rental while your car is in the shop
- **Towing** - pays to tow your car to a shop if it breaks down
- **New Care Replacement** - if your car is totaled (deemed too expensive to repair), the insurance company pays for the value of a new car rather than the depreciated value of your existing car. Some companies offer to reimburse the price of a car one-year newer than your car. Either way, you're paying extra for this type of coverage.

Not all of these options are necessary. For example, if you drive an older car, you're better off saving money rather than paying for comprehensive coverage. If you have a new car, chances are your vehicle manufacturer or dealer may offer free towing during the factory warranty period. If you own more than one car, you may not need to pay for rental reimbursement.

Obviously, the more options you add to a policy, the higher your premiums will be. Another way to reduce your premiums is to have higher deductibles. It's up to you to decide how to set those deductibles, but we don't recommend anything under $500. That's what your emergency expense account is for... pay yourself instead of the insurance company.

Homeowners Insurance. Homeowners insurance covers the physical structure and the personal property inside a home from *some* perils, like fire, hail, lightning, and theft. Notably, floods, sinkholes, and earthquakes are usually excluded–you have to get separate policies to cover those. Typically, a homeowners policy estimates the cost to rebuild the existing structure, and you specify a dollar value for the goods inside. Many homeowners undervalue their belongings because they don't really know how much they're worth or because they want to keep the cost of the policy down. The cost actually does not increase too much based on personal property, but there could be limits for certain classes of property and/or limits for each incident. If you have unique or very expensive items, you may want to consider an additional policy for them.

Renters Insurance. Renters insurance is also called **personal property insurance**. It covers the cost of replacing your belongings if they are damaged or stolen from your home. If you own a home, this is not necessary because homeowners insurance does the same, but you may want to consider a separate personal property insurance policy for big ticket items that may not be covered by homeowners insurance (e.g., engagement ring, antiques, collector items, etc.).

Mortgage Insurance. Mortgage insurance covers a lender in the case of default (i.e., you stop making payments on your mortgage). If you put less than 20% down on a house, you are required to purchase mortgage insurance. Note that you incur the cost for this policy, but you do not actually receive any benefits. That's another reason why we recommend not buying a house until you can afford to put at least 20% down. The mortgage insurance premium is automatically included in the mortgage bill, so many people are not even aware that they pay it.

Health Insurance. This topic is almost moot because of the Affordable Care Act. That said, there are many proposals to change the ACA, so we'll give you a little background. We don't intend to get into a policy discussion on the ACA or whatever replaces it. We will say, however, that before you get into a debate (or argument) on the subject, you should learn more about how insurance works and especially look into the problems that result from asymmetric information: adverse selection and moral hazard.

A **catastrophic plan** is pure insurance. You are paying the insurance company to cover unforeseen expenses such as broken bones, stitches, or treatments for newly-diagnosed diseases (often with a spending cap). Routine appointments like checkups or vaccinations would not be covered, and you pay for those yourself. Note also that having an existing condition is not something that would be covered by insurance, because if there is no uncertainty, there is no risk to manage. A problem that results is **adverse selection**: only those who expect to need insurance buy it, and when healthy people do not, the premiums rise, further driving out healthy people. This is one reason why the ACA mandates coverage.

A **healthcare plan** goes beyond insurance to cover routine items. The intention is to pool healthcare buyers and use their combined market power to negotiate lower prices. In reality, having a third-party cover expenses removes the rationing function of prices and causes people to over-consume healthcare services. This leads to rising costs and to non-price rationing of healthcare. So, while a healthcare plan can save you money, it also limits your choices. You may be restricted to certain doctors and procedures, and you may need to get pre-approval from the plan provider.

To help illustrate the difference between an insurance plan and a healthcare plan, go back to the car example. An auto insurance plan will cover unforeseen (and uncertain) events like accidents and theft, but it will not cover routine maintenance (oil changes and tire rotations) nor regular wear items (brakes, tires, and wiper blades). There are prepaid maintenance plans to cover scheduled maintenance, but these are more for convenience than saving money, and they also do not cover regular wear.[90] You can also purchase extended warranties

---

[90] Reed

and specific types of insurance (like road hazard protection for tires), but all of these deal with uncertain events and do not cover routine wear. An extended service plan that covers all expenses, including routine wear, is very difficult to find.[91] Yet automobiles are relatively simple compared to the human body. Why do we expect to find a reasonably priced plan to cover all our healthcare expenses, including normal wear and known future costs (i.e., pre-existing conditions)?

Life Insurance. The only reason to buy a life insurance policy is to provide financial security for your dependents in the unfortunate event that you die. If you are single with no dependents, you don't need much (if any) life insurance. If you are married with a stay-at-home spouse and three children under the age of ten, you need life insurance. But do not confuse life insurance with an investment. There are two basic types of life insurance policies: *term* policies and *cash-value* policies.

> **Term life insurance.** Term life insurance policies are pure insurance. You pay only for the insurance, and you get what you pay for. These policies pay your designated beneficiary in the case that you pass away. Obviously, premiums get more expensive as you get older (because the probability of passing increases). Many policies will require you to get a physical and may charge more if you engage in "risky" activities (like smoking). Also, most term life policies have disclaimers that they will not pay for certain types of death like suicide or being killed in combat.[92] In addition to term life policies, there are also **traumatic injury protection** policies which are similar but pay out in the event of a severe injury (losing a limb or an eye).

> **Cash-value insurance.** These types of policies are pitched by salesmen as investments as well as insurance. These policies go by many different names like whole life, universal life, and variable life policies. When you buy a

---

[91] Ford offers a "Ford Protect Premium Maintenance Plan" that does cover normal wear items (http://fordprotect.ford.com/premium-maintenance-plan). We were unable to find a similar plan from other automakers.

[92] Servicemembers Group Life Insurance (SGLI) is available for active duty military members and it does not have a "war clause."

cash-value policy, you are paying for more than just insurance. With these policies, you pay much larger premiums but after a period of time, your policy begins accumulating money, which you can later borrow or withdraw. On cash-value policies, part of your premium goes towards the actual insurance, while part is invested (actually, a big chunk in the early years usually goes to the insurance salesman as a commission). The problem is that the investment return on these insurance policies is typically abysmally low. A 1979 report by the Federal Trade Commission suggested that "whole life" policies provided an average return of only 1.3%.[93] Cash-value policies are expensive. In a 2000 study of cash-value policies, the average monthly premium for a $100,000 whole life policy was $110.97, compared to $7 for a comparable SGLI policy.[94] There is often a significant penalty if you terminate the policy early–indeed "early" can mean within the first 10 or 15 years of holding the policy. For example, Forster and Carson found that if an individual "cashed in" (terminated) his policy after just two years, the average cash-value policy returned just $100 even though he paid more than $2,000 in premiums.[95] On average, after ten years, the average cash surrender value was $8,074, even though the individual had paid more than $11,000 in premiums.[96] Because these policies are so expensive, it is not surprising that research found "approximately one-third of cash value policies lapse within the first five years."[97] People soon realize that they are better off terminating their cash-value policies and buying a cheap term life insurance policy instead.

Consumer Product Insurance. Almost any item you buy for more than $50 (especially electronics) offers some type of extended warranty or product replacement insurance. Most of the time, these policies are unnecessary. If it's a small dollar item (say, less than $500), you're probably better off saving the cost of the insurance. Many people get sucked into cell phone

---

[93] Carson and Forster, p32
[94] Carson and Forster, p36
[95] p42
[96] p42
[97] Carson and Forster, p39

insurance, which is usually required with discounted phones that are technically still owned by the carrier until they pay the phone off. These plans can be as much as $25 per month. You can easily shop around for plans that charge much less and still fulfill the carrier's requirement for insurance.

8.3. Our Recommendation

For any type of insurance, make sure you understand what is being sold. What will it *really* cost (premium and deductible)? How do you use it? Does it cover replacement or simply repair? Does it account for depreciation? Even if the insurance you are buying is required by law, make sure you shop around to find the best deal you can.

Remember the number one rule of gambling: The house always wins! When you buy insurance, you're trying to avoid the gamble. Make sure you understand what the gamble is and what the payoffs are, with and without insurance. Avoid over-insuring, which just guarantees the insurance company views you as a cash cow.

If we were not clear enough in the previous section, do not buy cash-value life insurance. Only buy term life insurance, and then only if you have dependents who will need to replace your income if you pass away. As you age and your investments grow in value, even term life insurance should be unnecessary.

Remember, your emergency expense account is also a form of insurance. You're frequently better off paying yourself instead of an insurance company.

Chapter 9. Making Big Purchases

In this chapter, we'll discuss making big purchases such as housing and transportation. These are big, not just in terms of the financial resources, but also because they have a big impact on your quality of life. There are other big purchases you will make in your life, including school for your kids or whether to even have kids. We can't answer all of these questions, but we hope the thought process presented here will help with other big decisions.

9.1. Housing

Everyone wants to own their own home. It's part of the American dream, and the most recent census reported nearly two-thirds (65.1%) of American households owned their home in 2010.[98] For many families, a home is a big part of their portfolio. According to the Federal Reserve, "home equity accounts for over 20 percent of total household net worth" in the U.S.[99] Whether a home is a good investment, however, is up for debate. There is a strong relationship between owning a home and accumulating wealth, but only for those who continue to own the home.[100] The driving factor is not just appreciating home prices, but more importantly, increased savings (by increasing equity through the principal portion of the mortgage payment).[101] That may be less true now with easy refinancing options that allow many people to "cash out" on home equity, essentially weakening the forced savings of a home mortgage.[102]

Before we get into a home as an investment, or even whether to rent or buy, let's discuss some quality of life aspects to selecting a home.

Rule 1: Location. There is a well-known joke that says the three most important considerations when buying a house are location, location, and location. This is usually in the context of

---

[98] "2010 Census Shows..."
[99] Li and Yao, p26
[100] Herbert, p48
[101] Herbert, pp48-49
[102] Li & Yang, p27

a specific city, with reference to purchasing a home in a nice neighborhood, with good schools, easy access to shopping, etc. However, it's also important to consider the city itself if you're moving there for a specific job (e.g., military assignment). How long is the job likely to last? Is it a major metropolitan area with a strong real estate market, or a rural area dependent on one or two major employers? These factors will affect resale value, so they are very important when deciding whether to rent or buy.

When considering location, here are a few factors to consider:

Commute. The length of your daily commute to work should be a huge consideration, in terms of both time and distance. You'll likely do this twice a day, five times a week. If you have a one hour commute, that's ten hours a week essentially wasted (unless you have a lot of audio books you're trying to catch up on). An important factor that you may not consider for commuting is direction. It's much nicer and easier to drive with the sun at your back rather than in your face, so a home east of your workplace is a great idea.

Traffic. Your commute is an obvious consideration, but overall traffic near your home is also important. The more traffic there is, generally, the less attractive a home will be. Less congestion typically will mean safer neighborhoods (strangers are more easily noticed), plus they are usually better for families with young children. In addition to the traffic density, consider the traffic patterns and the ease of entering and leaving your prospective neighborhood.

Age. Unless you're looking in a neighborhood with custom homes, which can vary greatly in age, most neighborhoods are tract housing, with all the homes built within a couple of years of each other. Therefore, settling on a location will lock you in to a certain age of house. This will greatly affect quality of life when you're actually in the home, rather than commuting. Newer houses are generally more spacious and energy efficient and require less maintenance. However, many people insist older houses are better built.

Yard. Many people like the idea of having lots of room, so they're not looking into the neighbor's windows (or vice versa). It's a nice thought, but realize larger lot sizes mean more expensive homes (even if the house itself is smaller). Consider how much time you'll actually spend enjoying the extra land... and how much time and expense you'll have to spend maintaining it. An apartment or condo removes the yard altogether and adds some benefits (lower cost, cheaper utilities), but close proximity to neighbors could offset the benefits. Condos also have high association dues to pay for landscaping and building insurance.

Surrounding Community. Beyond your immediate neighborhood, location will determine the distance and quality of schools. Even if you don't have kids, this is still important for resale purposes. You also want to consider other amenities around your home's location: access to parks, walking or jogging trails, grocery stores, and other shopping. This is obviously very dependent on what your interests are, but you should also look at what's around that you may not use yourself. For example, if there are clubs and bars around your neighborhood, you can expect a lot of late night noise. Similarly, a major highway or a bus or train station could create a lot of unwanted noise. A rural location may sound peaceful, but then you have to worry about wild animals and many more bugs than an urban setting (plus a longer drive to restaurants, entertainment, etc.). We're not suggesting every location is bad, just trying to make you aware of tradeoffs you may not have considered.

Orientation. Beyond the location of the house, the orientation is something to consider for quality of life. If you live in a heavy snow area, you probably do not want your driveway facing north because it will always be covered with snow or ice. If the house has a lot of west-facing windows, you will get a lot of hot afternoon sun. This can be good in the winter but increase your bills in the summer. South-facing windows are great if you live up north because you get a lot of sun in the winter to heat the home, without much sun in the summer.

Rent or Buy? Once you've settled on an area where you want to live, you have to decide whether to buy or rent. The biggest consideration should be how long you plan to live in the area. The shorter the stay, the less sense it makes to buy. Consider the expenses of buying a house: Typical realtor fees run between 3 and 6% on the sale of a house. According to Bankrate.com, the average closing cost on a mortgage for a $200,000 house is $2,128.[103] Even going with the lowest commission (3%), the home has to appreciate over $8,000 to make up for these costs. This is a lower bound because the estimate does not include other buying fees (title insurance, title search fees, taxes, property insurance, association fees), and we haven't even considered the costs of selling the home. Even with an appreciating housing market, we recommend not buying a house unless you will live in it for at least five years.

What about the tax benefit of owning a home? Mortgage interest and property taxes are deductible on your federal income taxes. Usually, these allow tax payers to itemize deductions to lower their taxable income more than simply using the standard deduction. Despite this, studies show the home mortgage interest deduction is only a big benefit to higher-income taxpayers (over $200,000 AGI).[104] Let's look at an example to see what this benefit really adds up to.

Assume you buy a $200,000 home with a 20% down payment and finance the remaining $160,000 with a 30-year fixed-rate mortgage at 4%. Let's also assume (generously) that you make $100,000 AGI, so you're in the 25% tax bracket. Your mortgage payment will be $763.86, and the interest paid in the first month is $533.33.[105] Rather than a full payment table, let's use a best case of $6,400 annual interest.[106] Even with $3,000 in property taxes, this still doesn't add up to the standard deduction for married filing jointly ($12,600).[107] If we further assume you

---

[103] "How Much House Can I Afford." Bankrate.com. This average is based on 20% down payment and includes fees charged by lenders and third-party fees for appraisals and credit reports. Average closing costs by state are available at the website.
[104] Li and Yang, p28
[105] Excel function "=PMT(.04/12,30*12,-160000)" (see Appendix E)
[106] Actual interest paid in the first year will be $6,348.71. This drops below $6,000 starting in year 4.

donated 10% of your AGI to charity, now your itemized deduction exceeds the standard deduction by $19,400 − 12,600 = $6,800. Your savings, however, is based on your marginal tax rate, so it is only 0.25 x $6,800 = $1,700. Saving $1,700 sounds good, but don't forget, you had to spend over $8,000 (on top of the purchase price) just to buy the house. In this example, you'll need five years of tax savings to offset the purchase costs.

So talking about tax savings on a home is a lot like bragging about saving money on stuff you bought on sale. In both cases, the amount you spent greatly exceeds any savings. Go back and look at that monthly payment again: $763.96. If you take the full 30 years to repay the mortgage, that $200,000 house will actually cost you $314,991.21.[108] That's over $100,000 in interest payments. Your $1,700 annual tax savings will not offset that money.

There are plenty of other costs involved with home ownership that make the numbers above worse. If you are renting a home, most repairs are the responsibility of the landlord (unless you caused the damage or signed a lease that makes you responsible for upkeep). If you have good handyman skills and enjoy making your own repairs, home ownership will be cheaper and might be something you enjoy. There are frequent small annoying expenses like broken sprinkler heads or leaky faucets. Even dead appliances, which can set you back hundreds of dollars, are nothing compared to major homeowner expenses. Putting new shingles on a roof (roughly every 20 to 30 years) will cost thousands of dollars. A new air conditioner or furnace (roughly every 12 to 15 years) is also in the thousands. You may even be as unlucky as one of your authors and get to re-plumb the entire house because of continual leaks from bad copper pipes under the concrete foundation. That's about $5,000 for a three bedroom, two bathroom house, if you're curious.

Of course, there are some benefits to owning your own home. We're not just talking about quality of life issues (yards, pets, garages, etc.). Arguments about a house over an apartment

---

[107] 1040 p2
[108] $40,000 + ($763.96 x 12 x 30) = $314,991.21

don't apply here because you can easily rent a house. The big benefit to owning your own home is having a portion of the payment go towards the **equity** in the home (i.e., the difference between what the home is worth and what you owe on the mortgage). If you are renting, the money you spend is gone forever. Plus your landlord can raise your rent whenever the lease is renewed. When you buy a house, your mortgage payment is fixed and will eventually be zero (assuming you sign a fixed-rate loan). If you sell the house for more than you owe, you will get some of the money from your monthly payments back.

In the end, we really can't tell you whether you should buy or rent. You can analyze the financial pros and cons for days, but a lot of the numbers are just guesses about the future. In general, renting is cheaper and more convenient in the short run, but buying can be a good investment if you will be living in the home for a long time. Just remember to keep your total housing expense (mortgage or rent plus insurance and utilities) below 28% of your monthly income. Also, do not buy too much house, so that you cannot afford to invest money in other areas. You should still ensure that you are saving and investing money for your retirement, your children's college education, etc.

Real Estate as an Investment. What about all those people who say buying a home is a good investment? Most of these are simply looking at the differences between purchase prices and selling prices (usually when the market is appreciating). They ignore a lot of the costs associated with homeownership. A collection of papers resulting from the 2001 symposium hosted by Harvard's Joint Center for Housing Studies concluded that alternative investments offer higher returns than home ownership.[109] They also noted that many home sales result in losses after accounting for inflation.[110] One study put the long-term real rate of return to home ownership at *negative* 0.5%.[111]

---

[109] Herbert, p2
[110] Herbert, p1
[111] Yi and Yang, p27

Gregory White, from *Business Insider*, likens home speculation to commodities markets, where the long-term expected return is 0%. "In the end, what makes money is human ingenuity—building new things and creating value. Things like rocks, or a constructed house that's wasting away every year in need of repairs is not where the money is."

That's not to say a house cannot be a good investment. There is evidence that a house can be a hedge against other assets, since the correlation coefficients between the S&P 500 and several housing price indices are negative.[112] You can also take advantage of investment leverage in a home, which could improve returns, but that works in both directions. Consider the $200,000 home with a 20% down payment from before. You only spend $40,000 up front. If the home appreciates by 20% to $240,000, you've earned a 100% return (ignoring all other costs and payments and inflation). However, if the home value drops by 20%, you lose your entire down payment if you sell the house.

When some people talk about real estate investments, they are talking about rental properties. The discussion above does not apply here because there are additional cash flows from a rental property that can improve the rate of return. There are things to consider before jumping into to rental properties. First, consider the market where the house will be. Is there a steady stream of qualified renters? Are you prepared to be a landlord and arrange for repairs when needed? Being an out-of-area landlord gets expensive, since most professional property managers charge a fixed percentage and then also get paid for any repairs they schedule (plus the cost of the repairs themselves). Even if you are local and make the repairs yourself, it only takes one major repair on a rental property to eat away any returns you may make on it. That said, some people do make a living off rental properties. Just do your homework and make sure you know what you're getting yourself into.

Realtors. In his bestselling book, *The Only Investment Guide You'll Ever Need*, Andrew Tobias devotes a chapter to the topic

---

[112] Yi and Yang, p28

of incentives called "Trust no one." How people behave in a business or financial arrangement depends largely on their incentives. You really need to understand everyone's incentives to understand a business deal. If you are working with a realtor, the realtor may be a "buyer's agent" or a "seller's agent." In truth, however, the realtor is ultimately concerned with his or her own interests more than those of either the buyer or the seller. For realtors, this means closing the deal. If realtors collectively earn a 6% commission on the sale of a house, they earn much more money if they close two houses quickly with two customers than if they spend a long period of time negotiating a $5,000 better deal for a single customer in the same length of time.

No matter how nice and helpful your realtor is, almost certainly his or her primary concern is matching buyers and sellers as often as possible. We're not knocking realtors. They can be helpful in buying and selling a home. But remember that everyone responds to incentives. A realtor is going to do their best to close the sale as quickly as they can, even if it means you might pay a little more for the house you're buying, or you might earn a little less on the house you are selling. That is usually the realtor's prime incentive–remember Andrew Tobias's advice.

9.2. Transportation

Teaching at the Air Force Academy, we frequently had students ask for car buying advice since all cadets were able to take "career starter" loans (previously called car loans). This is one place where your authors disagree. Rich is a traditional economist. That means he's a cheapskate who buys a used car and drives it until the wheels fall off. Len is a car snob whose car buying philosophy is best expressed by an old commercial: "Any car will get you where you want to go. A great car gets you there with a smile." He's the type who checked whether the GI Bill covered racing school. That said, the former perspective is the more rational choice for a healthy financial future. A good compromise: buy the cheapest car you're willing to live with.

Of course, buying a car may not even be necessary. There are other transportation options, such as public buses, taxis, bicycling, and even walking. Unless you're living in a dense urban area, however, chances are you'll need a car to get to get to work, buy groceries, and otherwise live your life. Here are some things to consider when looking for a car:

Car vs. Truck. You'll note we keep talking about cars rather than the more general "automobiles" or "vehicles" or saying "cars and trucks." Most people do not actually *need* a truck, and you'll find they are more expensive to own and operate than a car. Other than towing and off-roading, there are very few things that a truck can do that cannot be done better (and cheaper) by a car. If your job (or ego) requires you to drive a truck, just realize it's going to cost you more. (Plus, a higher center of gravity and greater curb weight saps all the fun out of driving.)

Practicality. Ideally, the car you purchase will be with you for several years. Unless you know for sure that there will be no changes in your life situation, you should get a car that is practical. For example, having a small, two-seat convertible will not work if you plan on having kids. A less dramatic example: if you buy a rear-wheel-drive sports car, it could be a problem if you then have to take a take a job in a snowy location. (Not that you can't, but you'll have to be a really good driver and/or get a separate set of tires for the winters.) Sadly, practical cars aren't sexy and cool. Sedans and wagons are rarely seen on posters or magazine covers. Don't fret–if you're someone who doesn't view a car as an appliance, there are plenty of affordable, practical options that have good driving dynamics... they just don't usually sell in high volumes, so you'll need to shop around. And remember, driving a slow car fast is a lot more fun than driving a fast car slow. Translation for the lawyers: Driving a fast car at *legal speeds* is usually not very rewarding; a responsive car with lower top-end speed and traction limits can be more fun in daily use... just ask an owner of a Camaro with the annoying 1-to-4 skip shift "feature."

Insurance Cost. Speaking of fast cars, they are almost always more expensive to insure, especially for younger drivers. From personal experience, insurance for a performance model can run up to $800 more per year than the base model of the same car. Before settling on a specific car, you should get insurance quotes for all the options you're considering to help you make an informed decision.

Maintenance Cost. For maintenance, we're referring to all operating costs. This includes fuel economy, type of gas, service intervals and costs, and other repair costs. Does the car you're looking at require premium fuel? You can figure that'll cost about $200 more per year.[113] A car that averages 35 mpg will save you about $340 a year over a car that averages 25 mpg.[114] Typically, American-branded cars are cheaper to service and repair because parts are more readily available. Maintenance and repairs for Asian-branded cars are slightly more expensive, and German brands are obscenely expensive. You can review all kinds of data on car reliability and service costs from various automotive websites. For example, Edmunds.com offers a "True Cost to Own" feature that estimates the five-year cost of a vehicle, factoring in depreciation, interest on financing, taxes and fees, insurance, fuel, maintenance, and federal tax credits.[115]

New vs. Used. Once you've settled on a specific car, there's the question of whether to buy one new or used. Most economists and financial advisors will always tell you to buy a used car because a new car experiences a lot of depreciation as soon as you drive it off the dealer lot. However, the lemon law (in economics, not the legal one) says that used cars are only available for sale because they are below average quality. That is, people who know their car exceeds the average value will not offer their car for sale (or trade in). Many dealerships now have certified pre-owned programs that offer warrantees with their used cars, so the asymmetric information problem is

---

[113] Assuming 10,000 miles per year with 25 mpg car and $0.50 price difference for premium gas: (10,000miles/25mpg) x $0.50/gal = $200; You'll note that some "premium" brands require premium gas even though their specific output (hp/L) is lower than mass-market brands that require regular gas.
[114] Assuming 10,000 miles per year and $3/gal gasoline
[115] Reed

mitigated. That said, there's no substitute for new car smell... just be aware of how much it will cost you.

Buy vs. Lease. Neither of us is a proponent of leasing a car, although it can make financial sense, depending on your situation and your preferences. On the one hand, you should not go into debt for a depreciating asset (like a car). When you lease a car, you're simply renting it, effectively only paying for the depreciation. If you insist on getting a new car every two or three years, leasing may be a cheaper option than buying. Just be sure you understand all the costs and limitations of the lease. Typically, a lease involves a down payment and a monthly charge. Leases may include free maintenance, which is good, but they definitely have mileage restrictions, frequently with heavy penalties if you exceed them. As we keep saying, make sure you know what you're getting into.

How to Buy. As a buyer, more information is always better. There are plenty of car buying and reviewing services. In addition to traditional car magazines and *Consumer Reports*, you can use TrueCar, Edmunds, Cars.com, CarsDirect, or CarBuyingTips.com (to name a few). We recommend you use these to help make your decision and to help make your purchase. Some buying sites get discounts for volume, while others essentially take bids from competing dealerships. You don't need to worry about your negotiation skills or high pressure sales tactics from a dealership. These sites allow you to make competition work for you so you can get the best price available... all while sitting in the comfort of your home.

Dealer Shenanigans. Finally, take the time to learn everything you can before you walk onto a dealership or talk to a sales person, and treat anything they say with suspicion... think "trust, but verify." We don't mean to impugn all dealerships or salesmen, but sometimes stereotypes exist for a reason. Don't be disrespectful, but realize these people live the car business and you're likely only paying attention for a brief period of time (once every few years or less). There is a huge information asymmetry that gives the dealership an edge in the transaction and prevents the market from being efficient. That hurts consumers (i.e., you pay more). Fortunately, the information age makes it easier to learn from the mistakes of others. Alex

Davies from *Business Insider* summarizes the 21 most common car buying scams taken from a list of 112 on RealCarTips.com. We can summarize it in even less space:

1. **Do your homework away from the dealership.** It only takes about 30 minutes of serious research to actually learn more about the car than most sales people know. You can learn about all the options and specifications direct from the manufacturer's website, which will also show any rebates or incentives available, and even let you search dealer inventories to locate the exact model you want.[116] (Some shadier dealers will keep these rebates for themselves if the consumer is not aware of their availability.) Your homework also includes how you're going to pay for the car. Check your bank's (and other banks') rates in addition to the manufacturer's offers. Often, manufacturers will offer the option of cheaper financing or cash rebates.[117] You can use the math in Appendix E to help figure out which option is the best deal. You should also know what your trade-in is worth. Treat selling your used car as a separate transaction from buying your next car.

2. **Focus on price.** Don't be tricked by questions about what you can afford, what you want your payment to be, or "what's it going to take to get you in this car today." Some dealers will confound consumers by changing the terms or topics of conversation. They'll try to simultaneously talk about the price, down payment, monthly payment, and trade-in value (if any). Once you've picked the car you want, the only thing you should be talking about is your out-the-door price, which you should already know from your research (ref "How to Buy" above). Dealers that try to get you to focus on a specific payment can manipulate the interest rate and/or term of the loan to make you pay much more than you should. Also, they may grant your price, but

---

[116] Where the particular model is located isn't that important because dealers trade cars with each other all the time. Pick the dealership you want to work with and let them figure out how to get the exact car you want. (Although picking a car off the lot may help you get a better deal.)

[117] These incentives are only for new models. Sadly, manufacturers don't try to bribe you to buy the used cars because only the dealership makes money on those.

then lowball your trade or claim the price is contingent on the trade. Don't fall for that. Treat your used car as a separate transaction. Even after you settle on the price, always watch for dealer add-ons to the price when it comes time to sign the paperwork.

3. **Don't rush.** Finally, your best negotiation tactic (aside shopping the competition) is being willing to walk away. Never let the dealer know you're wedded to a specific car or timeline. If you are desperate to get into a car immediately, the dealer will more than likely stand firm and not concede to any of your demands. (This is why many of their offers have an expiration to give you a false sense of urgency.) Again, be respectful, but stand firm. If the dealer will not do what you want, there are plenty of other dealerships you can work with if you make the time to do it right. Taking a couple extra days to buy your car could save you hundreds or thousands of dollars.

Appendix A. Military Compensation

Military members are paid twice a month by the Defense Finance and Accounting Service (DFAS). Military pay and allowances are established by Congress. General information about military pay can be found at the DFAS website: www.dfas.mil. Members of the military can get specific information about their pay and allowances at the secure "myPay" website: https://mypay.dfas.mil.

A military pay statement is called a "Leave and Earnings Statement," better known as an LES. The LES provides information on entitlements, deductions, allotments, taxes, and leave. The myPay website provides information about how to read your LES, as well as how to make changes online to various allotments in your monthly pay.

Your **entitlements** are your monthly pay and allowances. While all pay is taxable, most allowances are **tax-exempt**, which means a larger portion of your money is given to you rather than Uncle Sam. Here are some of the most common entitlements (pay) military officers receive, starting with the big three: Basic Pay, Basic Allowance for Subsistence (BAS), and Basic Allowance for Housing (BAH).

Basic Pay. Basic pay will make up the bulk of your paycheck each month. Basic pay is computed based on your rank and years of military service. Unfortunately, the four years as a service academy cadet do not count toward years of service. Basic pay is subject to state and federal income taxes. As a point of reference, as of January 2017 the monthly basic pay for lower ranks are shown in the table below: [118]

---

[118] You can get updated numbers at
https://www.dfas.mil/militarymembers/payentitlements/military-pay-charts.html

Pay Grade	Years of Service			
	2 or less	Over 2	Over 4	Over 6
O-3	$4,046.70	$4,587.00	$4,950.90	$5,398.20
O-2	$3,496.50	$3,982.20	$4,586.10	$4,741.20
O-1	$3,034.80	$3,159.00	$3,818.70	$3,818.70
E-5	$2,278.20	$2,431.50	$2,549.10	$2,669.10
E-4	$2,088.90	$2,195.70	$2,314.80	$2,432.10
E-3	$1,885.80	$2,004.30	$2,125.80	$2,125.80
E-2	$1,793.40	$1,793.40	$1,793.40	$1,793.40
E-1	$1,599.90	$1,599.90	$1,599.90	$1,599.90

For example, the basic pay of a second lieutenant (O-1) with less than two years of service was $3,034.80. Annual pay raises for military members are linked to the Employment Cost Index (ECI), which is tracked and published by the Bureau of Labor Statistics (www.bls.gov). Starting in 2007, military pay raises are automatically set to equal the annual increase in the ECI unless Congress intervenes by specifically authorizing a higher or lower pay increase.[119]

Basic Allowance for Subsistence (BAS). Military members get BAS to pay for meals. It is adjusted annually to follow changes in the USDA food cost index.[120] There are two different BAS rates—one for officers and one for enlisted. The last published (2017) monthly BAS rate for officers was $253.63 and $368.29 for enlisted. You will almost always receive a BAS allowance in your monthly LES—unless you are deployed and receiving rations from the military at your deployed location. In that case, since the military is providing you with delicious meals already, your BAS may be eliminated. One great thing about BAS is that it is tax-exempt, so you take home the entire BAS allowance.

Basic Allowance for Housing (BAH). BAH is a tax-exempt payment to defray the cost of housing in the area around your duty station. Privatized housing on base will charge the exact amount of your BAH. If you choose to live off-base, you may

---

[119] DFAS FAQ BP003. More topics at https://corpweb1.dfas.mil/askDFAS
[120] DFAS FAQ ET002

have to pay more (or less) than your BAH. Your BAH is a function of three things: rank, dependent status, and assigned permanent duty station. Since BAH is based on your permanently assigned duty station, if you deploy, your BAH rate does not change.[121]

You can visit www.defensetravel.dod.mil/site/bahCalc.cfm to find your BAH allowance (or check what it will be at your next duty station). For example, as of January 2017, the BAH allowance for a 2nd lieutenant, without dependents, assigned to the Air Force Academy was $1,350. If the lieutenant has dependents, the USAFA BAH rate is $1,563. (All that matters is whether the military member has dependents, not the actual number of dependents.) Since BAH is adjusted on the 1st of January, it is possible that average housing costs in your location could decline from one year to the next. To prevent unexpected out-of-pocket expenses for military members, BAH allowances include a "rate protection" so your BAH allowance may increase, but will not decrease as long as you do not PCS to a new location, change dependent status, or suffer a reduction in rank. BAH often does not cover the entire cost of a member's housing in the private sector and your actual expenses will depend greatly on the type of housing you choose (apartment, condo, single family home, etc.) and the location of that housing. For lieutenants without dependents, BAH rates are computed under the assumption the Lt will live in a 2-bedroom apartment. For captains without dependents, the BAH rate is computed for a 3-bedroom townhouse. For lieutenant colonels with dependents, the BAH rate is computed for a 4-bedroom single family detached home.[122]

Finally, it should be noted that BAH allowances are provided for military members permanently assigned to duty locations in the United States. Military members assigned overseas receive the Overseas Housing Allowance (OHA) in lieu of BAH to cover their housing costs.

---

[121] DFAS FAQ ET001
[122] BAH Primer at http://www.defensetravel.dod.mil/Docs/perdiem/BAH-Primer.pdf

In addition to the big three pay and allowances listed above, there are a variety of other types of compensation you may be entitled to receive, depending upon your duty assignment. A full list of incentive pay types can be found at militarypay.defense.gov/Pay/Special-and-Incentive-Pays/ Index. Here are a few of the more common incentives received by Air Force officers:

Aviation Career Incentive Pay (ACIP). ACIP is a career incentive pay for members on aviation duty. Commonly known as "flight pay," ACIP payments are based on a member's years of aviation service, in accordance with the table below.[123]

| Aviation Career Incentive Pay | |
Years of Aviation Service (includes flight training)	Monthly Amount
2 or less	$125
Over 2	$156
Over 3	$188
Over 4	$206
Over 6	$650
Over 14	$840
Over 22	$585
Over 23	$495
Over 24	$385
Over 25	$250

If an officer is assigned to duty in which he is actively flying, he automatically receives ACIP payments. However, later in their USAF careers, many officers will be assigned to staff jobs that do not require operational flying. In those instances, the officer will continue to receive ACIP payments as long as he or she has met the required "gates" of aviation service. For example, an officer who has

---

[123] http://www.military.com/benefits/military-pay/special-pay/aviation-career-incentive-pay-for-officers.html

been assigned to eight years (96 months) of operational flying duties before reaching the 12th year of aviation service is eligible to receive flight pay through 18 years of service, regardless of assigned duties, if he or she is still physically qualified for flying.

Foreign Language Proficiency Pay (FLPP). An officer who has been certified as proficient in a foreign language within the last 12 months may receive FLPP if the language has been identified by the Air Force as a "critical" need. The highest pay a military member may receive for a single language proficiency is $500 per month. The maximum FLPP for proficiency in multiple languages is $1,000 per month.[124] The military member must complete language testing annually (at the base education office) to continue receiving FLPP.

Family Separation Allowance (FSA). The FSA is meant to defray additional costs incurred by families when the military member is away for extended periods. For example, FSA helps pay the costs of home maintenance that may have to be contracted, which the military member might otherwise do if he or she were at home. As of April, 2007, the FSA allowance was $250 per month (prorated at $8.33 per day) and is only paid to military members who are TDY or deployed away from their permanent duty station *continuously* for 30 days or more.[125]

Hostile Fire/Imminent Danger Pay (IDP). Imminent Danger Pay is paid for military members serving in a designated IDP area. Hostile Fire Pay (HFP) is paid when military members are subjected to hostile fire or explosions or are in close proximity to them (as certified by "appropriate commanders"). Hostile fire pay is $225 per month and is not prorated (you get the full amount if you are only in the combat zone for one day). The IDP rate varies by location and, as of 2012, is prorated rather than

---

[124] http://www.military.com/benefits/military-pay/special-pay/foreign-language-proficiency-and-proficiency-bonus.html
[125] https://www.dfas.mil/militarymembers/payentitlements/fsa.html

paid for the entire month. You cannot receive both HFP and IDP.[126]

Hazardous Duty Incentive Pay (HDIP). HDIP is paid to military members who perform the following duties as part of their military jobs:

- flying duties as a non-crew member
- parachute jumping
- demolition of explosives
- handling toxic fuels
- experimental stress duty or flight deck duty

A service member can receive up to two different types of HDIP if the performing more than one duty. The table below shows HDIP rates as of 2017.[127]

Pay Grade	Amount	Pay Grade	Amount
O-4	$250	E-5	$190
O-3	$175	E-4	$165
O-2	$150	E-3	$150
O-1	$150	E-2	$150
		E-1	$150

In addition to the pay and allowances just discussed, military members have a generous retirement system. First, they have a pension plan, which is backed and funded by the federal government itself. After 20 years of active duty service, military retirees earn a pension for life. That's a pretty nice deal! While it's a very generous system, many military members do not serve for 20 years, so they do not benefit from the pension. In 1986, Congress created a 401(k) type of retirement plan for federal employees, known as the Thrift Savings Plan (TSP).[128] In 2001, the Thrift Savings Plan was also made available to

---

126

https://www.dfas.mil/militarymembers/payentitlements/specialpay/hfp_idp.html
[127] http://militarypay.defense.gov/Pay/Special-and-Incentive-Pays/HDIP/
[128] "Your TSP Account," p16.

military members, so today you can participate in your own 401(k)-style plan for the military.

Retirement System. One of the best parts of military compensation is a defined-benefit retirement system. There are two systems: "High-3" and "CSB/REDUX." Service members have to make a choice between these two programs at the 15-year point in their career. The programs have substantial differences, so it is important to understand each program before making your decision. DFAS provides calculators to help service members decide between the plans.[129]

High-3. At the twenty-year point, this program pays 50% of the average basic pay you earned for the highest three years of your career. For each additional year between 20 and 30, you earn an additional 2.5% of basic pay, so if you retired at 26 years, you would earn 65% of your average basic pay for the highest three years of your career (50% + 2.5% × 6 = 65%). In addition (and this is a very important point), your retirement pay is indexed for inflation by automatic annual Cost of Living Adjustments (COLAs) equal to the Consumer Price Index (CPI). That means that if the CPI goes up by 3% in a year, then your retirement pay is increased equally by 3%, to keep up with the increased cost of living.

CSB/REDUX. The Military Retirement Reform Act of 1986 (Public Law 99-348) was an attempt to reduce the benefits of a retirement system seen by some to be too generous and to create an incentive for military members to stay longer on active duty.[130] This 1986 Act created the "Redux" retirement system. Instead of paying 50% of basic pay at twenty years, Redux pays just 40% at twenty years, then pays an additional 3.5% per year after that, so at thirty years of service, retired pay is 75%, just as it is with the High-3 system. However, unlike the High-3 system, the COLAs for Redux are smaller, equal to the CPI minus 1% each year, with a provision for a one-time catch-up COLA when the retiree reaches age 62. In addition, at age 62, the

---

[129] https://www.dfas.mil/retiredmilitary/plan/estimate.html
[130] Henning, pCRS-2.

formula returns to the "50% + 2.5% per year past twenty" computation used in the High-3 system, but Redux COLAs after age 62 remain CPI minus 1%. In 1999, the Joint Chiefs of Staff asked Congress to repeal Redux, believing the reduced benefits were causing retention problems in the military.[131] Congress responded by repealing compulsory Redux. Today, military members reaching the 15-year point in their active military career are given a choice to opt for either the High-3 system or to accept a $30,000 Career Status Bonus (CSB) and fall under the Redux retirement system.

The best choice depends upon each member's financial situation and goals when they reach the 15-year point. For most people, the wealth-maximizing choice will probably be the High-3 system. But those with needs for immediate cash (e.g., college tuition for children) may prefer the CSB/Redux system—just realize that there is a significant retirement pay penalty later in life if you opt for the CSB payment.

Thrift Savings Plan (TSP). Information on the TSP can be found at the website www.tsp.gov. There is an option to invest in a traditional (*pre-tax*) plan or a Roth (*after-tax*) plan, although any contributions made from a war zone (and gains from those contributions) are automatically tax-free. For both types, the annual contribution limit in 2017 is $18,000.

Military members can enroll in the TSP program easily, using the secure myPay website.[132] When you enroll, you simply enter the percentage of basic pay, incentive pay, special pay or bonuses that you want withheld from your paycheck. If you want to take contributions from your special pay, incentive pay, or bonus pay, then you must first elect to have contributions taken from your basic pay. For simplicity, it's probably easiest to just take all of your TSP contributions from your basic pay. So if you are a 2Lt earning $3,034.80 per month in basic pay and you signed up to have 10% of your basic pay withheld for your TSP account, each month DFAS would set aside $303.48

---

[131] Smith, p308.
[132] https://mypay.dfas.mil/mypay.aspx

of your pre-tax pay into your TSP account. This is a great idea for two reasons:

1. The money is withheld before you receive your paycheck, so you don't have a chance to spend it. Forced savings discipline can be a very good thing if you have trouble sticking to a budget.

2. The money withheld for TSP is in pre-tax dollars. That means the amount of your take-home pay will drop by less than $303.48. Here's how it works: Suppose you are in the 15% marginal tax bracket. That means, for each additional dollar of income you are paid, the federal government takes 15 cents in income tax. With a $303.48 contribution, your monthly after-tax take-home pay will only be reduced by $303.48 x 0.85 = $257.96. You still get to take home $2,776.84 each month, and you get the satisfaction of knowing you have already done your saving for retirement.

Now let's assume you are smart enough to open a TSP account and set aside money each month for your retirement savings. What do you do with that money? The TSP program gives you several different funds where you can invest this money. Here's a brief description of each of the TSP funds:[133]

- **G Fund (Government Securities).** Invests in short-term U.S. Treasury bills

- **F Fund (Fixed Income Index).** Invests in a broad mix of U.S. bonds using the Bloomberg Barclays U.S. Aggregate Bond Index

- **C Fund (Common Stock Index).** Invests in stocks of large and medium-sized U.S. companies using an S&P 500 index

- **S Fund (Small Cap Stock Index).** Invests in stocks of small and medium-sized U.S. companies using the Dow Jones U.S. Completion TSM Index

---

[133] "Your TSP Account," p7.

- **I Fund (International Stock Index).** Invests in international stocks to match the MSCI EAFE (Europe, Australasia, Far East) Index

- **L Funds (Lifecycle Funds).** A family of funds with allocations in G, F, C, S, and I funds targeted to different retirement dates

Like other tax-deferred retirement accounts, TSP is meant for long-term investment until you retire (which means 59 ½ years old or later). While you can withdraw funds from your TSP account before you turn 59 ½ under certain narrowly defined "hardship" conditions, in most cases you'll pay a penalty if you try to get your money out before you reach retirement age. That's probably a good thing, so you won't be tempted to raid your retirement account for that new convertible or 4K TV you've been thinking about. TSP is also portable, so if you leave the military, you can take your TSP funds with you. You can leave it in a TSP account or transfer it to a 401(k)-style account elsewhere. (These are the only options that avoid a penalty.) If you leave it in TSP, you can no longer make contributions after you leave federal service.

Appendix B. Income Tax Example

The fictitious (and incomplete) W-2 below is used to complete the IRS Form 1040EZ on the next page.

a Employee's social security number		
	Safe, accurate, FAST! Use *e~file*	Visit the IRS website at www.irs.gov/efile
OMB No. 1545-0008		

b Employer identification number (EIN)	1 Wages, tips, other compensation: $36,417.60	2 Federal income tax withheld $3,641.00
c Employer's name, address, and ZIP code	3 Social security wages $36,417.60	4 Social security tax withheld $2,257.89
	5 Medicare wages and tips $36,417.60	6 Medicare tax withheld $528.06
	7 Social security tips	8 Allocated tips
d Control number	9	10 Dependent care benefits
e Employee's first name and initial Last name Suff.	11 Nonqualified plans	12a See instructions for box 12
	13 Statutory employee / Retirement plan / Third party sick pay	12b
	14 Other	12c
		12d
f Employee's address and ZIP code		

15 State	Employer's state ID number	16 State wages, tips, etc.	17 State income tax	18 Local wages, tips, etc.	19 Local income tax	20 Locality name
FL						

Form **W-2** Wage and Tax Statement   **2016**   Department of the Treasury—Internal Revenue Service

Copy B—To Be Filed With Employee's FEDERAL Tax Return.
This information is being furnished to the Internal Revenue Service.

The tax on line 10 comes from the tax table on the next page. The difference between this amount owed and the tax already paid (Federal income tax withheld, W-2 box 2) is the refund this tax filer will receive.

Department of the Treasury—Internal Revenue Service

Form 1040EZ

Income Tax Return for Single and Joint Filers With No Dependents (99) **2016**

OMB No. 1545-0074

Your first name and initial	Last name	Your social security number
If a joint return, spouse's first name and initial	Last name	Spouse's social security number
Home address (number and street). If you have a P.O. box, see instructions.	Apt. no.	▲ Make sure the SSN(s) above are correct.
City, town or post office, state, and ZIP code. If you have a foreign address, also complete spaces below (see instructions).		**Presidential Election Campaign** Check here if you, or your spouse if filing jointly, want $3 to go to this fund. Checking a box below will not change your tax or refund. ☐ You ☐ Spouse
Foreign country name	Foreign province/state/county	Foreign postal code

Income

Attach Form(s) W-2 here.

Enclose, but do not attach, any payment.

1	Wages, salaries, and tips. This should be shown in box 1 of your Form(s) W-2. Attach your Form(s) W-2.	1	36,417
2	Taxable interest. If the total is over $1,500, you cannot use Form 1040EZ.	2	500
3	Unemployment compensation and Alaska Permanent Fund dividends (see instructions).	3	
4	Add lines 1, 2, and 3. This is your adjusted gross income.	4	36,917
5	If someone can claim you (or your spouse if a joint return) as a dependent, check the applicable box(es) below and enter the amount from the worksheet on back. ☐ You ☐ Spouse If no one can claim you (or your spouse if a joint return), enter $10,350 if single; $20,700 if married filing jointly. See back for explanation.	5	10,350
6	Subtract line 5 from line 4. If line 5 is larger than line 4, enter -0-. This is your taxable income. ▶	6	26,567

Payments, Credits, and Tax

7	Federal income tax withheld from Form(s) W-2 and 1099.	7	3,641
8a	Earned income credit (EIC) (see instructions)	8a	
b	Nontaxable combat pay election.	8b	
9	Add lines 7 and 8a. These are your total payments and credits. ▶	9	3,641
10	Tax. Use the amount on line 6 above to find your tax in the tax table in the instructions. Then, enter the tax from the table on this line.	10	3,523
11	Health care: individual responsibility (see instructions) Full-year coverage ✗	11	
12	Add lines 10 and 11. This is your total tax.	12	3,523

Refund

Have it directly deposited! See instructions and fill in 13b, 13c, and 13d, or Form 8888.

13a	If line 9 is larger than line 12, subtract line 12 from line 9. This is your refund. If Form 8888 is attached, check here ▶ ☐	13a	118
▶ b	Routing number	▶ c Type: ☐ Checking ☐ Savings
▶ d	Account number	

Amount You Owe

14	If line 12 is larger than line 9, subtract line 9 from line 12. This is the amount you owe. For details on how to pay, see instructions. ▶	14	

Third Party Designee

Do you want to allow another person to discuss this return with the IRS (see instructions)? ☐ Yes. Complete below. ☐ No

Designee's name ▶	Phone no. ▶	Personal identification number (PIN) ▶

Sign Here

Under penalties of perjury, I declare that I have examined this return and, to the best of my knowledge and belief, it is true, correct, and accurately lists all amounts and sources of income I received during the tax year. Declaration of preparer (other than the taxpayer) is based on all information of which the preparer has any knowledge.

Joint return? See instructions.

Keep a copy for your records.

Your signature	Date	Your occupation	Daytime phone number
Spouse's signature. If a joint return, both must sign.	Date	Spouse's occupation	If the IRS sent you an Identity Protection PIN, enter it here (see inst.)

Paid Preparer Use Only

Print/Type preparer's name	Preparer's signature	Date	Check ☐ if self-employed	PTIN
Firm's name ▶		Firm's EIN ▶		
Firm's address ▶		Phone no.		

For Disclosure, Privacy Act, and Paperwork Reduction Act Notice, see instructions. Cat. No. 11329W Form **1040EZ** (2016)

2016 IRS Tax Table from p81 of 1040 instructions. The tax owed by a single filer with taxable income between $26,550 and $26,600 is circled.

21,000

If line 43 (taxable income) is— At least	But less than	And you are— Single	Married filing jointly *	Married filing separately	Head of a household
		Your tax is—			
21,000	21,050	2,690	2,226	2,690	2,481
21,050	21,100	2,698	2,234	2,698	2,489
21,100	21,150	2,705	2,241	2,705	2,506
21,150	21,200	2,713	2,249	2,713	2,514
21,200	21,250	2,720	2,256	2,720	2,521
21,250	21,300	2,726	2,264	2,728	2,529
21,300	21,350	2,735	2,271	2,735	2,536
21,350	21,400	2,743	2,279	2,743	2,544
21,400	21,450	2,750	2,286	2,750	2,551
21,450	21,500	2,758	2,294	2,758	2,559
21,500	21,550	2,765	2,301	2,765	2,566
21,550	21,600	2,773	2,309	2,773	2,574
21,600	21,650	2,780	2,316	2,780	2,581
21,650	21,700	2,788	2,324	2,788	2,589
21,700	21,750	2,795	2,331	2,795	2,596
21,750	21,800	2,803	2,339	2,803	2,604
21,800	21,850	2,810	2,346	2,810	2,611
21,850	21,900	2,818	2,354	2,818	2,619
21,900	21,950	2,825	2,361	2,825	2,626
21,950	22,000	2,833	2,369	2,833	2,634

22,000

At least	But less than	Single	Married filing jointly *	Married filing separately	Head of a household
22,000	22,050	2,840	2,376	2,840	2,641
22,050	22,100	2,848	2,384	2,848	2,649
22,100	22,150	2,855	2,391	2,855	2,656
22,150	22,200	2,863	2,399	2,863	2,664
22,200	22,250	2,870	2,406	2,870	2,671
22,250	22,300	2,878	2,414	2,878	2,679
22,300	22,350	2,885	2,421	2,885	2,686
22,350	22,400	2,893	2,429	2,893	2,694
22,400	22,450	2,900	2,436	2,900	2,701
22,450	22,500	2,908	2,444	2,908	2,709
22,500	22,550	2,915	2,451	2,915	2,716
22,550	22,600	2,923	2,459	2,923	2,724
22,600	22,650	2,930	2,466	2,930	2,731
22,650	22,700	2,938	2,474	2,938	2,739
22,700	22,750	2,945	2,481	2,945	2,746
22,750	22,800	2,953	2,489	2,953	2,754
22,800	22,850	2,960	2,496	2,960	2,761
22,850	22,900	2,968	2,504	2,968	2,769
22,900	22,950	2,975	2,511	2,975	2,776
22,950	23,000	2,983	2,519	2,983	2,784

23,000

At least	But less than	Single	Married filing jointly *	Married filing separately	Head of a household
23,000	23,050	2,990	2,526	2,990	2,791
23,050	23,100	2,996	2,534	2,998	2,799
23,100	23,150	3,005	2,541	3,005	2,806
23,150	23,200	3,013	2,549	3,013	2,814
23,200	23,250	3,020	2,556	3,020	2,821
23,250	23,300	3,028	2,564	3,028	2,829
23,300	23,350	3,035	2,571	3,035	2,836
23,350	23,400	3,043	2,579	3,043	2,844
23,400	23,450	3,050	2,586	3,050	2,851
23,450	23,500	3,058	2,594	3,058	2,859
23,500	23,550	3,065	2,601	3,065	2,866
23,550	23,600	3,073	2,609	3,073	2,874
23,600	23,650	3,080	2,616	3,080	2,881
23,650	23,700	3,088	2,624	3,088	2,889
23,700	23,750	3,095	2,631	3,095	2,896

24,000

If line 43 (taxable income) is— At least	But less than	And you are— Single	Married filing jointly *	Married filing separately	Head of a household
		Your tax is—			
24,000	24,050	3,140	2,676	3,140	2,941
24,050	24,100	3,148	2,684	3,148	2,949
24,100	24,150	3,155	2,691	3,155	2,956
24,150	24,200	3,163	2,699	3,163	2,964
24,200	24,250	3,170	2,706	3,170	2,971
24,250	24,300	3,178	2,714	3,178	2,979
24,300	24,350	3,185	2,721	3,185	2,986
24,350	24,400	3,193	2,729	3,193	2,994
24,400	24,450	3,200	2,736	3,200	3,001
24,450	24,500	3,208	2,744	3,208	3,009
24,500	24,550	3,215	2,751	3,215	3,016
24,550	24,600	3,223	2,759	3,223	3,024
24,600	24,650	3,230	2,766	3,230	3,031
24,650	24,700	3,238	2,774	3,238	3,039
24,700	24,750	3,245	2,781	3,245	3,046
24,750	24,800	3,253	2,789	3,253	3,054
24,800	24,850	3,260	2,796	3,260	3,061
24,850	24,900	3,268	2,804	3,268	3,069
24,900	24,950	3,275	2,811	3,275	3,076
24,950	25,000	3,283	2,819	3,283	3,084

25,000

At least	But less than	Single	Married filing jointly *	Married filing separately	Head of a household
25,000	25,050	3,290	2,826	3,290	3,091
25,050	25,100	3,298	2,834	3,298	3,099
25,100	25,150	3,305	2,841	3,305	3,106
25,150	25,200	3,313	2,849	3,313	3,114
25,200	25,250	3,320	2,856	3,320	3,121
25,250	25,300	3,328	2,864	3,328	3,129
25,300	25,350	3,335	2,871	3,335	3,136
25,350	25,400	3,343	2,879	3,343	3,144
25,400	25,450	3,350	2,886	3,350	3,151
25,450	25,500	3,358	2,894	3,358	3,159
25,500	25,550	3,365	2,901	3,365	3,166
25,550	25,600	3,373	2,909	3,373	3,174
25,600	25,650	3,380	2,916	3,380	3,181
25,650	25,700	3,388	2,924	3,388	3,189
25,700	25,750	3,395	2,931	3,395	3,196
25,750	25,800	3,403	2,939	3,403	3,204
25,800	25,850	3,410	2,946	3,410	3,211
25,850	25,900	3,418	2,954	3,418	3,219
25,900	25,950	3,425	2,961	3,425	3,226
25,950	26,000	3,433	2,969	3,433	3,234

26,000

At least	But less than	Single	Married filing jointly *	Married filing separately	Head of a household
26,000	26,050	3,440	2,976	3,440	3,241
26,050	26,100	3,448	2,984	3,448	3,249
26,100	26,150	3,455	2,991	3,455	3,256
26,150	26,200	3,463	2,999	3,463	3,264
26,200	26,250	3,470	3,006	3,470	3,271
26,250	26,300	3,478	3,014	3,478	3,279
26,300	26,350	3,485	3,021	3,485	3,286
26,350	26,400	3,493	3,029	3,493	3,294
26,400	26,450	3,500	3,036	3,500	3,301
26,450	26,500	3,508	3,044	3,508	3,309
26,500	26,550	3,515	3,051	3,515	3,316
26,550	26,600	(3,523)	3,059	3,523	3,324
26,600	26,650	3,530	3,066	3,530	3,331
26,650	26,700	3,538	3,074	3,538	3,339
26,700	26,750	3,545	3,081	3,545	3,346

27,0

If line 43 (taxable income) is— At least	But less than
27,000	27,
27,050	27,
27,100	27,
27,150	27,
27,200	27,
27,250	27,
27,300	27,
27,350	27,
27,400	27,
27,450	27,
27,500	27,
27,550	27,
27,600	27,
27,650	27,
27,700	27,
27,750	27,
27,800	27,
27,850	27,
27,900	27,
27,950	28,

28,0

At least	But less than
28,000	28,
28,050	28,
28,100	28,
28,150	28,
28,200	28,
28,250	28,
28,300	28,
28,350	28,
28,400	28,
28,450	28,
28,500	28,
28,550	28,
28,600	28,
28,650	28,
28,700	28,
28,750	28,
28,800	28,
28,850	28,
28,900	28,
28,950	29,

29,0

At least	But less than
29,000	29,
29,050	29,
29,100	29,
29,150	29,
29,200	29,
29,250	29,
29,300	29,
29,350	29,
29,400	29,
29,450	29,
29,500	29,
29,550	29,
29,600	29,
29,650	29,
29,700	29,

Appendix C. 2014 BLS Consumer Expenditures

Table 5. Average Annual Expenditures and Characteristics (excerpts), pp20-22. www.bls.gov/opub/reports/consumer-expenditures/2014/pdf/home.pdf

Item	All	1 person	2 people	3 people
Income before taxes	$66,877	$33,487	$73,312	$80,481
Average People in household	2.5	1.0	2.0	3.0
Average Vehicles	1.9	1.0	2.1	2.2
Average annual expenditures	$53,495	$31,987	$57,429	$61,526
Food at home	3,971	2,101	3,860	4,723
Food away from home	2,787	1,536	3,045	3,189
Alcoholic beverages	463	322	603	455
Housing	17,798	12,348	18,280	19,924
Shelter	10,491	8,057	10,582	11,322
Owned dwellings	6,149	3,600	6,640	7,061
Rented dwellings	3,631	4,098	2,925	3,630
Other lodging	710	359	1,017	631
Utilities, fuels, & public services	3,921	2,448	4,070	4,596
Household operations	1,174	639	1,060	1,471
Housekeeping supplies	632	359	691	708
Household furnishings & equip	1,581	844	1,877	1,828
Apparel & services	1,786	802	1,754	2,285
Transportation	9,073	4,617	10,094	10,547
Vehicle purchases (net outlay)	3,301	1,470	3,807	3,576
Gasoline & motor oil	2,468	1,300	2,552	3,006
Other vehicle expenses	2,723	1,510	2,994	3,346
Public & other transportation	581	337	741	618

Item	All	1 person	2 people	3 people
Healthcare	4,290	2,517	5,398	4,704
Entertainment	2,728	1,622	2,991	3,025
Personal care products & srvs	645	400	718	729
Reading	103	71	140	100
Education	1,236	849	984	1,733
Tobacco products & supplies	319	232	336	407
Miscellaneous	782	602	751	1,052
Cash contributions	1,788	1,428	2,259	1,547
Personal insurance & pensions	5,726	2,540	6,214	7,108
Life & other personal insurance	327	136	413	396
Pensions & Social Security	5,399	2,405	5,802	6,712

Appendix D. Major U.S. Stock Indices

Dow Jones (DJIA)

Composed of 30 large, well-known, U.S. companies, covering all industries except transportation and utilities. The Dow Jones Industrial Average was first published in May 1896. The thirty selected companies in the index are chosen by the editors of *The Wall Street Journal*. This is the longest-standing measure of U.S. stock performance. Although it contains only 30 companies, it has been remarkably consistent over time at tracking the performance of the broader stock market. For more information, see the DJIA factsheet:
http://us.spindices.com/idsenhancedfactsheet/file.pdf?indexId=1720081

S&P 500 Index

Standard and Poor's 500 index consists of 500 big U.S. companies, each with a market capitalization of at least $2.5 billion (average $40B). Because of the large size of each company, the S&P 500 is considered the index for the "large cap" market. The S&P 500 index has been tracked since 1957 and is widely considered the "benchmark" of the U.S. stock market. For more information, see the factsheet:
http://us.spindices.com/idsenhancedfactsheet/file.pdf?indexId=340

Russell 2000 Index

In contrast to the S&P 500, the Russell 2000 index concentrates on the "small cap" segment of the U.S. stock market. It includes 2000 stocks, selected annually, from among smaller companies. In January 2017, the market capitalization of the companies tracked by the Russell 2000 index averaged $2.1B. For more information, see the Russell 2000 Index factsheet at:
http://www.ftse.com/Analytics/FactSheets/temp/c18f869d-800f-46a8-a05b-b74439198685.pdf

NASDAQ Composite

The NASDAQ composite index includes all domestic and international stocks listed on the NASDAQ stock exchange. NASDAQ (National Association of Securities Dealers

Automated Quotations) is an electronic stock market, trading the stocks of approximately 3,200 companies (about 335 are foreign companies). The NASDAQ is the big newcomer to stock markets, and it is the most active market, with about 2 billion shares of stock traded each day. The NASDAQ covers a broad spectrum of industries, but is most heavily weighted with "technology" stocks. For more information about the NASDAQ, see the corporate factsheet at:
https://indexes.nasdaqomx.com/docs/COMP_FS.pdf

Wilshire 4500 & 5000
These two indices are also managed by Dow Jones. The Wilshire 5000 represents the entire U.S. stock market. The Wilshire 4500 represents the entire market with the exception of those companies included in the S&P 500 index.
https://wilshire.com/indexinfo/pdf/Wilshire%205000/Wilshire%205000%20Fact%20Sheet.pdf

Appendix E. Financial Math

This book was not initially intended for a full-blown academic course, but we couldn't help ourselves. This appendix introduces most of the relevant financial equations to support several academic lessons on financial analysis or engineering economics.[134] This topic is also called **time-value of money**, and it helps to think of the dollar signs having subscripts for the years or time periods. That means you can't simply add and subtract dollars from different periods. You must first convert them into the same period. That should become clear as we look at moving money into the future (FV) and the present (PV), as well as adding general cash flows over different periods of time.

For the entire appendix, we will try to keep the notation as consistent as possible:

FV = future value
PV = present value
PMT = uniform payment (or investment) each period
r = annual interest rate; annual percentage rate (APR)
r_e = effective annual interest rate; annual percentage yield
m = number of periods of compounding per year
n = number of years of compounding

E1. Future Value Calculations

If you deposit $100 into an account that pays a fixed 4% interest each year, after one year you will have $104. That is computed by taking 4% of $100 and adding it back to the $100. Using some simple arithmetic, we get

$$\$100(0.04) + \$100 = \$100(0.04 + 1) = \$100(1.04)$$

If the money stays for another year, you get another 4%, but the second year starts with $104 or $100(1.04). Therefore, the value after the second year will be

---

[134] The appendix is based on the classroom handout: "Introduction to Financial Analysis and Engineering Economics" by Richard Fullerton and Jim Pocock, Nov 17, 2009.

$$\$100(1.04)1.04 = \$100(1.04)^2$$

If you follow this logic, after the compounding continues for n years, the future value becomes $\$100(1.04)^n$. The general formula to compute the **future value of an initial deposit** (PV) that grows at a constant annual rate (r) for n years is

$$FV = PV(1+r)^n \qquad (1)$$

Now suppose instead that this investment paid the 4% interest semiannually. That means it pays interest twice a year: $4\% \div 2 = 2\%$ after six months (half a year), and then the remaining 2% at the end of the year. If you think about it, the first year is really like two years at 2% interest so the value after one year is $\$100(1.02)^2$. If it paid the 4% interest quarterly, it would be paying $4\% \div 4 = 1\%$ four times throughout the year, so the value after one year is $\$100(1.01)^4$. The general formula to compute the future value of an initial deposit (PV) that grows at a constant annual interest rate (r) **compounded m times per year** for n years is

$$FV = PV\left(1+\frac{r}{m}\right)^{mn} \qquad (2)$$

Note that the constant annual interest rate (r) is quite misleading. It is sometimes called an **annual percentage rate (APR)**. It simply adds up the interest rate from each compounding period (e.g., $2\% + 2\% = 4\%$), but it does not distinguish between investments with different numbers of compounding periods. If we convert the APR into the effective annual interest rate, often called the **effective rate** (r_e) or **annual percentage yield (APY)**, it will account for the number of compounding periods (m) and will be a larger number as m increases.[135]

$$r_e = \left(1+\frac{r}{m}\right)^m - 1 \qquad (3)$$

---

[135] Make Equation (2) look like (1): $FV = PV(1 + r/m)^{mn} = PV(1 + r_e)^n$ with $r_e = (1 + r/m)^m$

Frequently, you'll see APR reported for credit cards or mortgage loans because it makes the interest rate appear smaller. For accounts where you receive the interest (savings accounts and CDs), you'll frequently see the APY quoted. It's important to know the difference. You can avoid the math by using the EFFECT function in Excel: "**=EFFECT(Nominal_ rate, Nper)**." *Nominal_rate* is the APR. *Nper* is the number of compounding periods, m.

Speaking of credit cards, many will do **continuous compounding** (i.e., $m \to \infty$). When this occurs, equation (2) becomes

$$FV = PVe^{rm} \qquad (4)$$

where e is the natural logarithm (2.71828).

Now suppose instead of an initial deposit, you make **regular, equal annual investments** at the end of each year (so they do not earn interest in the year invested). This is called an **annuity**. Let's see what this future value looks like. If you only have one payment (PMT), then $FV = PMT$ because there is no interest earned. If there are two payments, then $FV = PMT + PMT(1 + r)$. We can't really work with that yet. Let's add a third payment:

$$FV = PMT + PMT(1+r) + PMT(1+r)^2$$

If we follow this logic, for n payments, the future value will be

$$FV = PMT + PMT(1+r) + PMT(1+r)^2 \ldots + PMT(1+r)^{n-1} =$$

$$PMT\sum_{i=1}^{n}(1+r)^{i-1}$$

Now we can write the formula for the **future value of an annuity** that gets n equal annual investments at the end of each year (no interest in the year invested).[136]

---

[136] $\displaystyle\sum_{i=1}^{n}(1+r)^{i-1} = \frac{(1+r)^n - 1}{r}$ ... take our word for it or wolframalpha.com

$$FV = PMT\left(\frac{(1+r)^n - 1}{r}\right) \qquad (5)$$

If the annual investments are made at the start of the year, so they do earn interest the same year, the investment is called an **annuity due**. The future value modifies Equation (5) by multiplying each term by $(1 + r)$, adding an extra round of compounding to each investment:

$$FV = PMT\left(\frac{(1+r)^n - 1}{r}\right)(1+r) \qquad (6)$$

All of these future value calculations can be easily done in Excel with the function FV. The syntax is "**=FV(*Rate, Nper, Pmt*, [*Pv*], [*Type*]**)." *Rate* is the interest rate per period (r/m). *Nper* is the total number of periods (mn). *Pmt* is a constant payment made each period (for annuities and annuities due). *Pv* is an initial investment (optional). *Type* is an optional binary argument: 1 if payments are at the beginning of the period (so they accrue interest as in an annuity due); 0 (or omitted) if payments are at the end of the period. Like a financial calculator, Excel expects incoming cash flows to be positive and outgoing cash flows to be negative, but we don't need to worry about that yet. Just be aware that if you enter all the arguments as positive numbers, the FV returned will be negative. Let's try some sample problems.

Problem #1. Suppose you invest $100 today in a savings account that pays 4% annual interest. What will be the value of the account in 7 years?

  Solution: $FV = \$100(1.04)^7 = \$131.59$
  Excel: "=FV(0.04,7,0,-100)"

Problem #2. Suppose you invest $300 today in a savings account that pays 6% interest compounded quarterly (four times per year). What will be the value in the account in 27 months (2.25 years)?

Solution: $FV = \$300\left(1 + \dfrac{0.06}{4}\right)^{4(2.25)} = \$300(1.015)^9 = \$343.02$

Excel: "=FV(0.06/4,4*2.25,0,-300)"

Problem #3. What is the effective rate for the account described in Problem #2?

Solution: $r_e = \left(1 + \dfrac{0.06}{4}\right)^4 - 1 = 0.06136$

Excel: "=EFFECT(0.06,4)" or "=RATE(2.25,0,-300,343.02)"

Problem #4. Suppose $100 is invested at the end of each year in an account that pays 6% annual interest. These investments are made for 35 years. How much will the annuity be worth at the end of the 35-year period?

Solution: $FV = \$100\left(\dfrac{1.06^{35} - 1}{0.06}\right) = \$11,143.48$

Excel: "=FV(0.06,35,-100)"

Problem #5. Suppose the $100 in Problem #4 is invested at the start of each year, rather than the end. How much will the annuity due be worth at the end of the 35-year period?

Solution: $FV = \$100\left(\dfrac{1.06^{35} - 1}{0.06}\right)(1.06) = \$11,812.09$

Excel: "=FV(0.06,35,-100,0,1)"

Problem #6. Suppose the $100 in Problem #4 is spread out as a $50 investment twice per year in an investment that pays 6% interest compounded semiannually. How much will the annuity be worth at the end of the 35-year period?

Solution: $FV = \$50\left(\dfrac{1.03^{70} - 1}{0.03}\right) = \$11,529.70$

Excel: " =FV(0.06/2,35*2,-50)"

NOTE: This applies the same technique used to derive Equation (2) from Equation (1), but it is applied to Equation (5).

E2. Present Value Calculations

You can use fairly simple algebra to convert all the future value equations into present value equations. When going from a present value to a future value, we call it **compounding** (because you're compounding interest payments). When we go from a future value to a present value, we call it **discounting** (because we are effectively removing the interest).[137] The present value equations are more practical from a personal finance perspective because they can be used to tell you how much you need to invest today at a given interest rate to grow to a specified amount in the future. From Equation (1), we can solve the **present value of a future payment** n years in the future:

$$PV = \frac{FV}{(1+r)^n} \qquad (7)$$

If interest is compounded more frequently than once per year, as in Equation (2), we can apply the same technique to Equation (7) or simply solve Equation (2) to get the formula for the present value of a future payment n years in the future, discounted at a constant annual interest rate (r) **compounded m times per year**:

$$PV = \frac{FV}{\left(1+\dfrac{r}{m}\right)^{mn}} \qquad (8)$$

Equation (5) does not have a present value, but we can combine Equations (1) and (5) to find the present value of a

---

[137] Note there are many rates that can be used for discounting. Typically, an estimate of inflation is used for discounting, although we can use an individual's personal discount rate, which accounts for personal preference for consumption now rather than in the future. Warner and Pleeter estimate personal discount rates can be as high as 30% (p33).

series of equal annual payments for n years, which both grows and is discounted at a constant rate (r):[138]

$$PV = PMT\left(\frac{(1+r)^n - 1}{r(1+r)^n}\right) \qquad (9)$$

Recall that Equation (5) assumed the investments were made at the end of each year so they do not earn interest in the year invested. If instead, they are made at the beginning of the year (so they do earn interest), the formula becomes

$$PV = PMT\left(\frac{(1+r)^n - 1}{r(1+r)^{n-1}}\right) \qquad (10)$$

Equation (9) is one of the most practical formulas for personal finance because it can be used to determine the amount of money you need to have when you retire to support a certain lifestyle. In this case, PMT is the amount of money you plan to withdraw from your investments each year and PV is the total value of your investments when you retire.[139] In this case we're looking at PV as a value in the future, but it is the present value at the time of retirement. Hopefully, this will be cleared up when we discuss cash flows in the next section. Whether you use Equation (9) or (10) is only important for an academic class. In reality, you likely won't be making the full investment at a single point during the year, and you definitely will not be getting the exact same return with certainty every year. We'll address that in Section E6.

---

[138] Substituting Equation (1) into Equation (5) results in

$$PV(1+r)^n = PMT\left(\frac{(1+r)^n - 1}{r}\right)$$

[139] If the investments grow at a constant rate (r), but you discount at a different constant rate (d), Equations (9) and (10) would be

$$PV = PMT\left(\frac{(1+r)^n - 1}{r(1+d)^n}\right) \text{ and } PV = PMT\left(\frac{(1+r)^n - 1}{r(1+d)^n}\right)(1+r)$$

You can solve Equation (9) for PMT in terms of PV, n, and r to determine the required minimum **payment for a simple interest loan**:

$$PMT = PV\left(\frac{r(1+r)^n}{(1+r)^n - 1}\right) \qquad (11)$$

Another very practical personal finance formula mirrors Equation (11) but comes from Equation (5). We can rearrange terms to solve for PMT. That gives the value of **regular, equal annual investments** at a constant return, r, needed to grow to a specific amount of money n years in the future:

$$PMT = FV\left(\frac{r}{(1+r)^n - 1}\right) \qquad (12)$$

So you can use Equation (9) to determine how much you need to have at retirement, then use Equation (12) to determine how much you need to save each year in order to grow your investments to that value. (Equations (11) and (12) can be modified as we did (5) and (9) to account for the investments/payments earning interest in the year they are made.)

A final present value formula is the value of an annuity payment that will be received forever (also called a **perpetuity**). This formula is used by various methods for estimating the value of a stock. We won't get into them, but these techniques assume a company continues to operate forever, and they use this formula to estimate the present value of the company's future cash flows. If the perpetuity is discounted at a constant rate (r), the present value is

$$PV = \frac{PMT}{r} \qquad (13)$$

All of these present value calculations can be easily done in Excel with the function PV. The syntax is "**=PV(Rate, Nper, Pmt, [Fv], [Type]**)." *Rate* is the interest rate per period (r/m). *Nper* is the total number of periods (mn). *Pmt* is a constant payment made each period (for annuities and annuities due). *Fv* is the future value (optional). *Type* is an optional binary argument just like the FV function (1 if payments are at the beginning of the period; 0 (or omitted) if payments are at the end of the period). There's also an Excel function for PMT. The syntax is "**=PMT(*Rate, Nper, Pv, [Fv], [Type]*)**." The arguments are the same as the PV and FV functions. For any of the Excel functions, you can approximate perpetuities by using a very large number for *Nper*.

Let's try some sample problems.

Problem #7. How much money do you need to set aside today, at 6% annual interest, in order to have a $40,000 deposit to use as a down payment on your first house purchase in 10 years?

Solution: $PV = \dfrac{\$40,000}{(1.06)^{10}} = \$22,335.79$

Excel: "=PV(0.06,10,0,-40000)"

Problem #8. ACME Industries has a pension plan for its employees. To be fully funded, the pension plan must have $50 million in the fund 12 years from now. The pension fund manager believes he can earn 7.5% annually on his investments. How much money does ACME need to have in the pension fund today to be fully funded?

Solution: $PV = \dfrac{\$50}{(1.075)^{12}} = \$20.99$ million

Excel: "=PV(0.075,12,0,-50)"

Problem #9. Suppose you win a lottery that gives you a choice of receiving $7,500 today or receiving $1,000 per year for the next 10 years. If you discount future payments at 5% per year, which payment would you prefer to receive?

Solution: $PV = \$1,000\left(\dfrac{(1.05)^{10}-1}{0.05(1.05)^{10}}\right) = \$7,721.73$

Excel: "=PV(0.05,10,-1000)"
Since the PV of the payments exceeds $7,500, you should opt for the payments.

Problem #10. Based on your research, you think you need $80,000 per year to live comfortably. If you plan to live off your retirement for 35 years (age 65 to 100), how much must your total investments be worth when you retire if your investments earn a constant 4% return? (Assume you do not continue to save after retirement, but only withdraw exactly $80,000 at the end of each year.)

Solution: $PV = \$80,000 \left(\dfrac{(1.04)^{35} - 1}{0.04(1.04)^{35}} \right) = \$1,493,169.06$

Excel: "=PV(0.04,35,-80000)"

Problem #11. Suppose you retire at age 60 with a nest egg of $1 million. If you continue to earn a guaranteed 5% return on this money over the course of the next 30 years, how big can your regular annual withdrawals be until the fund is depleted? (Assume withdrawals are at the end of the year.)

Solution: $PMT = \$1M \left(\dfrac{0.05(1.05)^{30}}{(1.05)^{30} - 1} \right) = \$65,051.43$

Excel: "=PMT(0.05,30,-1000000)"

Problem #12. You're now 20 years old, and you want to reach that $1 million nest egg at age 60. How much do you need to save each year at a 5% return in order to reach your goal in 40 years? (Assume investments are at the end of the year.)

Solution: $PMT = \$1M \left(\dfrac{0.05}{(1.05)^{40} - 1} \right) = \$8,278.16$

Excel: "=PMT(0.05,40,0,-1000000)"

Problem #13. Suppose a benefactor wants to give back to his alma mater and donates $2 million to establish an endowed chair. If the university earns a 5% return on the endowment, how much money can they pay each year to this professor without ever touching the $2 million principal?

Solution: $PMT = \$2M(0.05) = \$100,000$

Excel: " =PMT(0.05,9999,-2000000)"

NOTE: This requires rearranging the terms in Equation (11)

E3. Cash Flows

All of the formulas we've looked at so far have been pretty restrictive because they've used constant interest rates or constant payments. What if either of these is not constant? For more complicated problems, it's easier to consider the cash flows in each period and then apply the appropriate formulas multiple times. The first step is to properly track the cash flows. This can be done with a **cash flow diagram**. The diagram uses arrows on a time line to show revenues (cash in) and expenditures (cash out), scaled to the magnitude of the payments. Revenue arrows are drawn facing upward, while expenses are drawn facing downward. If you draw every cash flow individually, you can usually simplify the diagram by adding the cash flows in the same time period. (You can easily track the cash flows in a spreadsheet without the diagram, but we cover the diagram because it is used in the Fundamentals of Engineering (FE) exam.)

Let's look at an example to illustrate the concept. Suppose a company wants to purchase a new truck for $26,000 up front. Maintenance will run $1,000 per year, and the truck will generate revenues of $7,000 per year for its projected life of 5 years. The salvage value of the truck after 5 years is projected to be $5,000. This scenario is represented below with a cash flow diagram (full and simplified) and a spreadsheet:

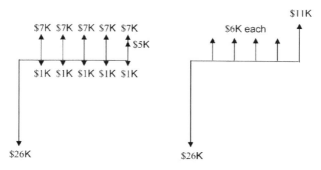

Time	Inflow	Outflow	Net flow
0	0	−26000	−26000
1	7000	−1000	6000
2	7000	−1000	6000
3	7000	−1000	6000
4	7000	−1000	6000
5	7000 + 5000	−1000	11000

Let's try some sample problems.

Problem #14. Suppose the company above can lease the truck for five years. The lease has a $10,000 down payment now and $4,000 payments for each of the next 5 years. At the end of the lease, the company returns the vehicle for no residual value. The lease includes maintenance costs. Revenue generation remains $7,000 per year. Draw and simplify the cash flow diagram.

Solution:

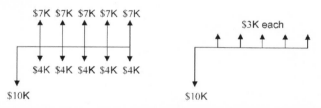

Time	Inflow	Outflow	Net flow
0	0	−10000	−10000
1	7000	−4000	3000
2	7000	−4000	3000
3	7000	−4000	3000
4	7000	−4000	3000
5	7000	−4000	3000

Problem #15. A piece of equipment costs $4,000. The equipment will earn $1,500 per year in rent payments. After 4 years the equipment will be scrapped and sold for a salvage value of $1,000. Annual maintenance costs are $500. Draw and simplify the cash flow diagram.

Solution.

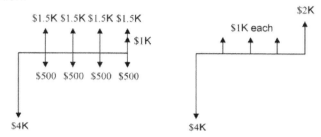

Time	Inflow	Outflow	Net flow
0	0	−4000	−4000
1	1500	−500	1000
2	1500	−500	1000
3	1500	−500	1000
4	1500 + 1000	−500	2000

E4. Comparison of Alternatives

Once you know the cash flows for a particular project or investment, you can apply a couple of techniques to compare the project to other alternatives. The first technique simply applies Equation (7) to the cash flow in each time period to convert them into present values. Once these values are in the same "units" (i.e., dollars in the same time period), they can simply be added together to determine the **net present value** (*NPV*) of the entire series of cash flows, which is the total monetary value of the project. The project with the greatest *NPV* is the best alternative. Let's look at the truck purchase vs. lease example from the previous section using a discount rate of 6% (and rounding to the nearest dollar).[140]

---

[140] A company making this comparison would use its **weighted average cost of capital (WACC)** to discount the cash flows. The WACC is essentially the "cost" of money for a company because it's the rate at which the company

	Purchase:	**Lease:**
Year 0:	$PV = -\$26,000$	$PV = -\$10,000$
Year 1:	$PV = \dfrac{\$6,000}{(1.06)^1} = \$5,660$	$PV = \dfrac{\$3,000}{(1.06)^1} = \$2,830$
Year 2:	$PV = \dfrac{\$6,000}{(1.06)^2} = \$5,340$	$PV = \dfrac{\$3,000}{(1.06)^2} = \$2,670$
Year 3:	$PV = \dfrac{\$6,000}{(1.06)^3} = \$5,038$	$PV = \dfrac{\$3,000}{(1.06)^3} = \$2,519$
Year 4:	$PV = \dfrac{\$6,000}{(1.06)^4} = \$4,753$	$PV = \dfrac{\$3,000}{(1.06)^4} = \$2,376$
Year 5:	$PV = \dfrac{\$11,000}{(1.06)^5} = \$8,220$	$PV = \dfrac{\$3,000}{(1.06)^5} = \$2,242$
NPV	**$3,011**	**$2,637**

Therefore, with a 6% discount rate, the best alternative is to purchase the truck because it yields the greatest net present value for the associated cash flows.

These calculations can be done in Excel using the NPV function. The syntax is "**=NPV(Rate, Value1, [Value2],...)**." *Rate* is the discount rate, and you can enter values individually or as a range. Excel assumes *Value1* starts in period 1, so you need to add any cash flow in time 0 first. For example, the syntax for the purchase option would be: "=26000 + NPV(0.06, 6000, 6000, 6000, 6000, 11000)." Alternatively, if you have the cash flows in the range B3:B8 (B3 is 26000, B4 is 6000, etc.), the syntax would be "=B3 + NPV(0.06,B4:B8)."

A problem with comparing alternatives using present values is that the results can change with different discount rates when the cash flows differ widely. The difference could be either in the number of periods (one project much longer than the other) or in the magnitude of the cash flows (one project has much larger cash flows). This example has the latter problem because the time zero cash flow is over twice as large for the purchase option. Let's repeat the example with an 8% discount rate.

---

borrows money.

	Purchase:	**Lease:**
Year 0:	−$26,000	−$10,000
Year 1:	$PV = \dfrac{\$6,000}{(1.08)^1} = \$5,556$	$2,778
Year 2:	$5,144	$2,572
Year 3:	$4,763	$2,381
Year 4:	$4,410	$2,205
Year 5:	$7,486	$2,042
NPV	**$1,359**	**$2,637**

Now the lease appears to be the better alternative. This happens because a higher opportunity cost for money (i.e., higher interest rate) means money further out in the future has less value. In this case, the higher future cash flows for the purchase option do not sufficiently offset the larger initial cost as they did with a 6% discount rate.

Another way of comparing alternatives is to compare their respective **internal rates of return (IRR)**, also commonly known as the investment's **yield**. Both truck scenarios above require an up-front investment followed by a stream of cash flows in subsequent years. The internal rate of return for each investment is the interest rate that would need to be earned on the initial investment to return enough income to just pay off the cash flow stream. In other words, the IRR is the discount rate that makes the *NPV* equal zero. The equation for computing the Internal Rate of Return (or yield) is as follows:

$$\sum_{i=0}^{n} \frac{C_i}{(1+r)^i} = 0 \qquad (14)$$

$$C_0 + \frac{C_1}{(1+r)^1} + \frac{C_2}{(1+r)^2} + \frac{C_3}{(1+r)^3} + \ldots + \frac{C_n}{(1+r)^n} = 0$$

Where C_i is the cash flow in time i. The discount rate, r, that solves the equation is the project's IRR. You can solve it by hand with awesome algebra skills or use trial and error or (highly recommended) use a computer program. The Excel function IRR works. The syntax is "**=IRR(*Values*, [*Guess*])**." *Values* is a range that contains the cash flows starting in period zero. These are expected to be chronological with no missing periods, so zero cash flows must be included to account for all the periods. *Guess* is an optional argument that provides an initial estimate for Excel to work its magic.

For the purchase option above, if you have the cash flows in the range B3:B8 (B3 is 26000, B4 is 6000, etc.), "=IRR(B3:B8)" returns 9.79%. That means the *NPV* is zero when the discount rate is 9.79%. This is equivalent to investing the initial $26,000 in an account that pays $9.79% interest. If you withdrew money each year at the cash flow rates in the example ($6,000 each year), you would run out of funds with the final withdrawal of $11,000 in year 5. This latter example is simpler to understand, but IRR is not dependent on an initial investment. As long as there are both negative and positive cash flows, an IRR can be computed.

The IRR for the lease option is 15.24%. Therefore, using IRR as the decision criterion, the lease is the better option.

Let's try some practice problems.

Problem #16. You are planning to buy a new car and have narrowed your choice down to a particular model, but are torn between the regular gas version or the hybrid version. Both cars have the same features in terms of air conditioning, power windows/doors, stereo system, etc. However, the gas car costs $19,510 and gets a combined gas mileage of 34 mpg, while the hybrid costs $22,600 and gets a combined gas mileage of 50 mpg. Assume you expect to drive 12,000 miles per year and expect to keep the car for 10 years. Furthermore, you expect the cost of gasoline to be $3 per gallon over the life of your car. Using a discount rate of 5% per year, which is the better option? Ignore sales tax, licensing, fees, tax credits, maintenance costs, resale value, etc. Also, keep it simple and round to the nearest dollar.

> Solution: Since we only have expenses (no cash inflow), we cannot use IRR. Instead we pick the lowest present value. We must determine the cash flows for the gasoline expense:
> Gas: (12,000 miles ÷ 34 mpg) x $3/gal = $1,059

Hybrid: (12,000 miles ÷ 50 mpg) x $3/gal = $720
Realize the 10-year cash flows are just an annuity. You can find the *PV* using Equation (9) and then add that to the cost of the car.

Gas: $NPV = \$19,510 + \$1,059\left(\dfrac{(1.05)^{10}-1}{0.05(1.05)^{10}}\right) = \$19,510 +$

$\$8,177 = \$27,687$

Hybrid: $NPV = \$22,600 + \$720\left(\dfrac{(1.05)^{10}-1}{0.05(1.05)^{10}}\right) = \$22,600 +$

$\$5,560 = \$28,160$

With Excel:
Gas: "=19510+PV(0.05,10,-1059)"
Hybrid: "=22600+PV(0.05,10,-720)"
Under these assumptions, the gas car is the better option.

Problem #17. Compute the IRR for the equipment in Problem #15.

Solution: Excel: "=IRR(B2:B6)"

	A	B	C	D
1	Time	Net flow	IRR	
2	0	–4000	8.47%	
3	1	1000		
4	2	1000		
5	3	1000		
6	4	2000		

Problem #18. An investment costs $10,070 and provides a payment of $1,000 at the end of each year for 12 years. What is the interest rate yield (i.e., IRR) on this investment?

Solution: Use Equation (14) for IRR, but use Equation (9) for the present value of all the cash flows from years 1 to 12.

$$-\$10,070 + \$1,000\left(\frac{(1+r)^{12} - 1}{r(1+r)^{12}}\right) = 0 \text{ ... solve for } r \text{ using}$$

Excel: "=IRR(A1:A12)"
$r = 2.81\%$

	A	B
1	−10070	2.81%
2	1000	
3	1000	
4	1000	
5	1000	
6	1000	
7	1000	
8	1000	
9	1000	
10	1000	
11	1000	
12	1000	

E5. Bond Valuation

You now have enough knowledge of financial math to do basic bond valuations. Think of a bond as a series of cash flows. When you purchase the bond, you are spending money (a negative cash flow). In future years, the bond makes interest payments. These payments are essentially an annuity, and you can easily compute their present value. At maturity, the bond pays its par value. This is a future value you can discount to find the present value. If you do not know the price of the bond, this technique will tell you what the price should be. If there is a listed price for the bond, you can compute an IRR to determine if it is a good investment.

Let's try some practice problems.

Problem #19. Suppose a bond is selling at its par value of $1,000. It has a coupon rate of 6% and matures in 5 years. What is the interest rate yield (i.e., IRR) on this bond?

Solution: The cash flow to purchase the bond (at time zero) is –$1,000. The cash flow for the next 4 years is $1,000 x 0.06 = $60. In year 5, there is the same $60 interest payment, plus the par value of $1,000. The cash flows are shown below. Using Excel ("=IRR(A1:A5)"), the IRR is 6%.

	A	B
1	–1000	6.00%
2	60	
3	60	
4	60	
5	1060	

Problem #20. Suppose the bond in Problem #19 does not have a listed price and the market interest rate for investments of similar risk is 4%. What should this bond's price be?

Solution: Use Equations (7) & (9)

$$PV = \$60\left(\frac{(1.04)^5 - 1}{0.04(1.04)^5}\right) + \frac{\$1,000}{(1.04)^5} = \$1,089.04$$

Excel: "=PV(0.04,5,60,1000)"
NOTE: In this case, the bond is selling at a premium (above par) because the market rate is less than the coupon rate.

Problem #21. Suppose the bond in Problem #20 pays semiannual interest. That is, it pays $30 every six months. What should this bond's price be?

Solution: You have to convert the coupon and discount rates into semiannual rates (divide by 2) and double the number of periods:

$$PV = \$30\left(\frac{(1.02)^{10} - 1}{0.02(1.02)^{10}}\right) + \frac{\$1,000}{(1.02)^{10}} = \$1,089.83$$

Excel: "=PV(0.02,10,30,1000)"

Problem #22. Suppose a bond has a 4% coupon rate, $1,000 par value, 25-year maturity. If the bond is selling for $970, what is its yield to maturity (i.e. IRR).

Solution: This is the same as Problem #19 with cash flows: −$970 at time 0, $40 for years 1 to 24, and $1040 in year 25. You can solve this with Excel ("=IRR(A1:A25)"); the IRR is 4.2%. Another way that doesn't require entering all the cash flows is to use **Goal Seek**. In any cell type "=-PV(A1,25,40,1000)" (we're doing it in cell B1). This will calculate the price of the bond using whatever discount rate is currently in cell A1. Now go to the "Data" tab and select "Goal Seek..." from the "What-If Analysis" drop down. Complete the dialog box as shown on the right to have Excel determine the rate (in A1) required to set the present value computed in B1 equal to 970.

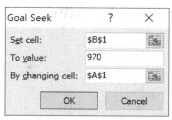

E6. Dealing with Uncertainty

Everything to this point has dealt with known, constant rates and payments. Other than bonds, which are contractually obligated (unless there's a bankruptcy), nothing in finance is certain. To paraphrase Sam Savage's "Flaw of Averages": Using an average return for financial planning means your answers will be wrong on average.[141] It ignores the variability (or risk) in the return. We don't want to turn this into a full-blown statistics course, but here are a couple of ways you can deal with the uncertainty:

Sampling. If you have historical data for the returns of a particular investment, you can set up a formula in Excel to randomly sample the historic returns. True, future returns won't necessarily follow these returns, but this technique at least allows you to replicate some of the variability in the returns. You can either draw the numbers "as is" or you can create a histogram and use the bins. The "as is" technique is simpler. If

---

[141] p11

you have 25 years of data, you simply have Excel give you a random number between 1 and 25 ("**=RANDBETWEEN(1,25)**"). Now use that value to pick the corresponding return from the historic list.

Distribution. If you have sufficient historical data to fit a distribution, or if you simply have an idea of what the distribution looks like, you can generate random returns utilizing the mean and standard deviation of the returns. Excel has built in functions for various distributions, but you'd most likely use a normal distribution ("**NORM.INV(*Probability, Mean, Standard_Dev*)**"). This function returns the value of a normal random variable corresponding to the specified *Probability* (which you'd generate with "**=RAND()**").

For both cases, these techniques will generate a single, random return. Use these to set up a model of your investment plan. Next you run thousands of iterations to develop a distribution for the objective of your model (e.g., retirement nest egg at age 65, value of nest egg during retirement, etc.).[142] You can do this in Excel with a **"Data Table..."** (under the "What-If Analysis" drop down in the "Data" tab).

Let's look at Problem #10 to see how this works. Recall that we determined you need roughly $1.5 million dollars at retirement in order to live off $80,000 per year for 35 years (with the investment continuing to grow at 4%). How likely is that to happen? It only takes one return less than 4% and your portfolio won't last all 35 years. On the other hand, one year with a really great return could make you consider spending more than $80K a year. Let's add a little uncertainty to simulate what might possibly happen and determine how often that $1.5M will last for 35 years. We'll use a normal distribution with an average return of 4% and a standard deviation of 3%. That only has a probability of a negative return roughly 9% of the time (and the same chance of getting a return greater than double the average).

The chart below shows the total portfolio value each year as it consistently drops from $1.5 million down to zero in year 35

---

[142] This is called a Monte Carlo simulation

(Certain Return). There are also five versions using the random returns. Some are clearly better, and some are worse. We ran 5,000 trials and found that over half the time (53%), the portfolio runs out of money before year 35. On average, when the portfolio runs out of money, it does so at year 30. It always lasted over 20 years. In very rare cases (0.6%), the portfolio value actually increased in value despite withdrawing all that money. Those must be some awesome investors!

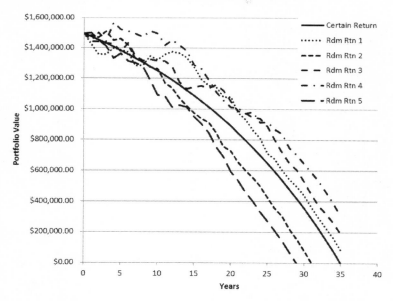

That's a fairly simple example, and we know we didn't cover exactly how to replicate what we did. Our point is not to turn this into a full-blown modeling lesson. We just want to emphasize that the previous formulas are really just "back-of-the-envelope," easy guesses to help you plan. Also, hopefully, this demonstrates why it's important to put your retirement savings in a safer investment (lower variation) as you approach retirement age.

E7. Equation Summary

Notation: FV = future value
          PV = present value
          PMT = uniform payment/investment each period
          m = number of periods of compounding per year
          n = number of years of compounding
          r = annual interest rate (APR)
          r_e = effective annual interest rate (APY)
          e = natural logarithm (2.71828)
          C_i = cash flow in year i

(1) Future value, annual compounding $\qquad FV = PV(1+r)^n$

(2) Future value, general compounding $\qquad FV = PV\left(1+\dfrac{r}{m}\right)^{mn}$

(3) Effective annual interest rate (APY) $\qquad r_e = \left(1+\dfrac{r}{m}\right)^m - 1$

(4) Future value, continuous compounding $\qquad FV = PVe^{rn}$

Future value of:

     (5) Annuity (PMT earns   (6) Annuity due (PMT does
     no int. when deposited)   earn int. when deposited)

$$FV = PMT\left(\frac{(1+r)^n - 1}{r}\right) \qquad FV = PMT\left(\frac{(1+r)^n - 1}{r}\right)(1+r)$$

(7) Present value, annual compounding $\qquad PV = \dfrac{FV}{(1+r)^n}$

(8) Present value, general compounding $\qquad PV = \dfrac{FV}{\left(1+\dfrac{r}{m}\right)^{mn}}$

Present value of:

     (9) Annuity   (10) Annuity due

$$PV = PMT\left(\frac{(1+r)^n - 1}{r(1+r)^n}\right) \qquad PV = PMT\left(\frac{(1+r)^n - 1}{r(1+r)^{n-1}}\right)$$

(Required nest egg to live off PMT in retirement)

Payments for:

(11a) Annuity PV

$$PMT = PV\left(\frac{r(1+r)^n}{(1+r)^n - 1}\right)$$

(11b) Annuity due PV

$$PMT = PV\left(\frac{r(1+r)^{n-1}}{(1+r)^n - 1}\right)$$

(Required payment for simple interest loan)

(12a) Annuity FV

$$PMT = FV\left(\frac{r}{(1+r)^n - 1}\right)$$

(12b) Annuity due FV

$$PMT = FV\left(\frac{r}{(1+r)^n - 1}\right)\left(\frac{1}{1+r}\right)$$

(Required annual savings to reach nest egg)

(13) Present value of perpetuity $PV = \dfrac{PMT}{r}$

(14) Net present value of cash flows $NPV = \displaystyle\sum_{i=0}^{n}\frac{C_i}{(1+r)^i}$

(15) Internal Rate of Return (Yield) r that solves $NPV = 0$

References

"All About Credit Reports." Annualcreditreport.com Internet article, Feb 3, 2017. https://www.annualcreditreport.com/whatIsCreditReport.action

"Aviation Career Incentive Pay for Officers." Military.com internet article, Jan 17, 2017, http://www.military.com/benefits/military-pay/special-pay/aviation-career-incentive-pay-for-officers.html

Baertlein, Lisa. "Chipotle Mexican Grill Profit Misses, Shares Fall." Reuters, Feb 14, 2008. http://www.reuters.com/article/rbssConsumerGoodsAndRetailNews/idUSN 1427564820080215?sp=true

Brownell, Matt. "The Surprising Downside of Cutting Up Your Credit Cards." AOL Finance, Jun 5, 2013. Internet article, Feb 3, 2017. https://www.aol.com/article/2013/06/05/cutting-up-credit-cards-bad-idea/20597579/

Carson, James and Mark Forster. "The Nature and Causes of Variation in Insurance Policy Yields: Whole Life and Universal Life." Journal of Insurance Issues. Vol 23, No 1. 2003.

Consumer Financial Protection Bureau. "How to Rebuild Your Credit." Internet article, Feb 3, 2017. https://pueblo.gpo.gov/CFPBPubs/CFPBPubs.php?PubID=13135

Damodaran, Aswath. "Annual Returns on Stock, T. Bonds and T. Bills: 1928-Current." Internet article, 19 Feb 2017. http://www.stern.nyu.edu/~adamodar/pc/datasets/histretSP.xls

Davies, Alex. "21 Scams Used By Devious Car Dealers–And How to Avoid Them." Business Insider, Sep 26, 2013. Internet article, Mar 3, 2017. http://www.businessinsider.com/how-to-avoid-21-car-dealer-scams-tricks-2013-9

Defense Finance and Accounting Service. "2017 Military Pay Tables." Internet article, Jan 10, 2017. https://www.dfas.mil/dam/jcr:0066b0ac-2d02-47a6-8b78-1cdc91b56ef7/2017MilitaryPayChart.pdf

--. "Family Separation Allowance." Internet article, Jan 17, 2017. https://www.dfas.mil/militarymembers/payentitlements/fsa.html

--. FAQ BP003. "How are annual pay raises calculated?" Internet article, Jan 10, 2017. https://corpweb1.dfas.mil/askDFAS/faqView?faq.faqId=223&pgModId=4

--. FAQ ET001. "What are the BAH Rates?" Internet article, Jan 10, 2017. https://corpweb1.dfas.mil/askDFAS/faqView?faq.faqId=237&pgModId=4

--. FAQ ET002. "What are the BAS Rates?" Internet article, Jan 10, 2017. https://corpweb1.dfas.mil/askDFAS/faqView?faq.faqId=233&pgModId=4

--. "Hazardous Duty Incentive Pay (HDIP)." Internet article, Jan 17, 2017. http://militarypay.defense.gov/Pay/Special-and-Incentive-Pays/HDIP/

--. "Hostile Fire/Imminent Danger Pay." Internet article, Jan 17, 2017. https://www.dfas.mil/militarymembers/payentitlements/specialpay/hfp_idp.html

Defense Travel Management Office. "A Primer on the Basic Allowance for Housing (BAH) for the Uniformed Services." Internet article, Jan 10, 2017. http://www.defensetravel.dod.mil/Docs/perdiem/BAH-Primer.pdf

Department of Labor, Bureau of Labor Statistics. Report 1063, "Consumer Expenditures in 2014." October 2016. Internet article, Jan 23, 2017. https://www.bls.gov/opub/reports/consumer-expenditures/2014/pdf/home.pdf

Department of the Treasury, Internal Revenue Service. Form 1040 2016. Internet article, Jan 10, 2017. https://www.irs.gov/pub/irs-pdf/f1040.pdf

--. Form 1040EZ 2016. Internet article, Jan 10, 2017. https://www.irs.gov/pub/irs-pdf/f1040ez.pdf

--. Form 1040 Instructions 2016. Internet article, Jan 10, 2017. https://www.irs.gov/pub/irs-pdf/i1040gi.pdf

--. Form W-2 2016. Internet article, Jan 10, 2017. https://www.irs.gov/pub/irs-pdf/fw2.pdf

--. Publication 525. "Taxable and Nontaxable Income" (for 2016 returns). Internet article, Feb 2, 2017. https://www.irs.gov/pub/irs-pdf/p525.pdf

--. Publication 590-A. "Contributions to Individual Retirement Arrangements (IRAs)" (for 2016 returns). Internet article, Feb 2, 2017. https://www.irs.gov/pub/irs-pdf/p590a.pdf

--. Publication 590-B. "Distributions from Individual Retirement Arrangements (IRAs)" (for 2016 returns). Internet article, Feb 2, 2017. https://www.irs.gov/pub/irs-pdf/p590b.pdf

--. Topic 306. "Penalty for Underpayment of Estimated Tax." Internet article, Jan 17, 2017. https://www.irs.gov/taxtopics/tc306.html

--. Topic 751. "Social Security and Medicare Withholding Rates." Internet article, Jan 17, 2017. https://www.irs.gov/taxtopics/tc751.html

Economic Report of the President, January 2017. Washington: Government Printing Office, 2017. Internet article, Feb 16, 2017. https://www.gpo.gov/fdsys/pkg/ERP-2017/pdf/ERP-2017.pdf

Elkins, Kathleen. "Here's How Much the Average Young Family Has Saved for Retirement." CNBC.com, Sep 12, 2016. Internet Article, Apr 1, 2017. http://www.cnbc.com/2016/09/12/heres-how-much-the-average-american-family-has-saved-for-retirement.html

Fama, Eugene. "Efficient Capital Markets: A Review of Theory and Empirical Work." The Journal of Finance. Vol 25, No 2, 1970.

Federal Reserve Bank of Boston. "Banking Basics." Nov 2011. Internet article, Aug 31, 2016. http://www.bos.frb.org/education/pubs/banking2.pdf

Federal Reserve Bank of Minneapolis. "Consumer Price Index, 1913-." Internet article, Feb 19, 2017. https://www.minneapolisfed.org/community/teaching-aids/cpi-calculator-information/consumer-price-index-and-inflation-rates-1913

"Foreign Language Proficiency Pay / Foreign Language Proficiency Bonus." Military.com internet article, Jan 17, 2017.

http://www.military.com/benefits/military-pay/special-pay/foreign-language-proficiency-and-proficiency-bonus.html

Henning, Charles A. "Military Retirement: Major Legislative Issues." Congressional Research Service Brief for Congress, Mar 14, 2006. Internet article, Feb 23, 2017. https://fas.org/sgp/crs/natsec/IB85159.pdf

Herbert, Christopher E, Daniel T. McCue and Rocio Sanchez-Moyano. "Is Homeownership Still an Effective Means of Building Wealth for Low-income and Minority Households? (Was it Ever?)" Joint Center for Housing Studies. Harvard University, Sept 2013. Internet article, Feb 22, 2017. http://jchs.harvard.edu/sites/jchs.harvard.edu/files/hbtl-06.pdf

Holden, Sarah; Ireland, Kathy; Leonard-Chambers, Vicky and Michael Bogdan. "The Individual Retirement Account at Age 30: A Retrospective." Investment Company Institute Perspective. Vol 11, No 1. Feb 2005. Washington, D.C. Internet article, Feb 2, 2017. https://www.ici.org/pdf/per11-01.pdf

"How Much Are Closing Costs In Your State?" Bankrate.com internet article, Mar 1, 2017. http://www.bankrate.com/finance/mortgages/closing-costs/closing-costs-by-state.aspx

"How Much House Can I Afford?" Bankrate.com internet article, Jan 10, 2017. http://www.bankrate.com/calculators/mortgages/new-house-calculator.aspx

Kawamoto, Dawn. "Amazon.com IPO Skyrockets" cnet.com news. May 15, 1997. Internet article, Jan 2, 2002. https://www.cnet.com/news/amazon-com-ipo-skyrockets/

Kuhle, James and Ralph Pope. "A Comprehensive Long-Term Performance Analysis of Load Versus No-Load Mutual Funds." Journal of Financial and Strategic Decisions. Vol 13, no 2, Summer 2000.

Laibson, David. "Gold Eggs and Hyperbolic Discounting." Quarterly Journal of Economics. May 1997.

Larimer, Rob. "Colorado Springs Utility Rate Proposal Compared to Other Cities." The Gazette. Nov 11, 2013. Internet article, Jan 23, 2017. http://gazette.com/colorado-springs-utility-rate-proposal-compared-with-other-cities/article/1509091

Li, Wenli and Fang Yang. "American Dream or American Obsession? The Economic Benefits and Costs of Homeownership." Business Review. Qtr 3, 2010. Federal Reserve Bank of Philadelphia. Internet article, Feb 23, 2017. https://www.philadelphiafed.org/-/media/research-and-data/publications/business-review/2010/q3/brq310_benefits-and-costs-of-homeownership.pdf?la=en

Li, Wenli and Rui Yao. "Your House Just Doubled in Value? Don't Uncork the Champagne Just Yet." Business Review. Qtr 1, 2006. Federal Reserve Bank of Philadelphia. Internet article, Feb 23, 2017. https://www.philadelphiafed.org/-/media/research-and-data/publications/business-review/2006/q1/q1_06_housevalue.pdf?la=en

Lyke, Bob. "Tax Benefits for Education in the Taxpayer Relief Act of 1997: New Legislative Developments." Congressional Research Service Report for

Congress. Sept 14, 2000.
http://www.senate.gov/~budget/democratic/crsbackground/edutaxben.pdf

Malkiel, Burton G. "The Efficient Market Hypothesis and Its Critics." The Journal of Economic Perspectives, Vol 17, No 1, 2003.

Mazzucco, Denise. "Historical CD Interest Rates - 1984-2016." Bankrate.com internet article, Feb 22, 2017. http://www.bankrate.com/finance/cd-rates-history-0112.aspx

Office of Consumer Protection, National Credit Union Administration. "How Your Accounts Are Federally Insured." March 2014. Internet article, Jan 30, 2017. https://www.ncua.gov/Legal/GuidesEtc/GuidesManuals/NCUAHowYourAcctInsured.pdf

Office of Management and Budget. "Analytical Perspectives Budget of the U.S. Government, Fiscal Year 2017." Internet article, Feb 7, 2017. https://www.gpo.gov/fdsys/pkg/BUDGET-2017-PER/pdf/BUDGET-2017-PER.pdf

Opdyke, Jeff. The Wall Street Journal Complete Personal Finance Guidebook. New York: Random House, 2006.

Peterson, Lars. "7 Simple and Free Budgeting Tools." U.S. News and World Report. Jan 14, 2015. Internet article, Jan 23, 2017. http://money.usnews.com/money/blogs/my-money/2015/01/14/7-simple-and-free-budgeting-tools

Reed, Philip. "How to Use Edmunds True Cost to Own." Edmunds.com, Jul 31 2014. Internet article, Mar 3, 2017. https://www.edmunds.com/car-buying/true-cost-to-own-tco.html

--. "Prepaid Maintenance Plans." Edmunds.com, Apr 30, 2009. Internet article, Mar 3, 2017. https://www.edmunds.com/car-buying/prepaid-maintenance-plans.html

"Resources for Renters." Gainesville Regional Utilities. Internet article, Jan 23, 2017. https://www.gru.com/TabID/3658/Default.aspx

Savage, Sam. The Flaw of Averages. Hoboken: Wiley & Sons, 2009.

Shen, Pu. "How Long is a Long-Term Investment?" Economic Review, 1st Qtr, 2005. Federal Reserve Bank of Kansas City, 2005. https://www.kansascityfed.org/PUBLICAT/ECONREV/PDF/1Q05Shen.pdf

--. "The P/E Ratio and Stock Market Performance." Economic Review, 4th Qtr, 2000. Federal Reserve Bank of Kansas City, 2000. https://www.kansascityfed.org/PUBLICAT/ECONREV/PDF/4Q00Shen.pdf

Smith, Marvin. "The Military Retirement Reform Act of 1986--or REDUX: A Postmortem." Journal of Political and Military Sociology. Vol 29, Winter 2001. pp305-318.

Sonders, Liz Ann. "Volatility and Complacency Make Strange Bedfellows." Charles Schwab On Investing. Summer 2007, ed. Jennifer Cronin. Phoenix: Charles Schwab, Inc.

"Special and Incentive Pay Index." Militarypay.defense.gov. Internet article, Jan 17, 2017. http://militarypay.defense.gov/Pay/Special-and-Incentive-Pays/Index/

Stanley, Thomas and William Danko. The Millionaire Next Door. New York: Simon and Schuster, 1996.

"State Individual Income Tax Rates and Brackets for 2016." TaxFoundation.org internet article, Jan 17, 2017. http://taxfoundation.org/article/state-individual-income-tax-rates-and-brackets-2016

"The Morningstar Rating for Funds." Morningstar.com, Oct 6, 2010. Internet article, 23 Feb 2017. http://corporate.morningstar.com/US/documents/MethodologyDocuments/FactSheets/MorningstarRatingForFunds_FactSheet.pdf

Thrift Savings Plan. "Your TSP Account: A Guide for Beneficiary Participants." Feb 2017. Internet article, Feb 2, 2017. https://www.tsp.gov/PDF/formspubs/tspbk33.pdf

TimeValue Software. "Tcalc Online Financial Calculators." Internet article, Jan 23, 2017. http://tcalc.timevalue.com/

Tobias, Andrew. The Only Investment Guide You'll Ever Need. New York: Harcourt, 2005.

Tyson, Eric. Personal Finance for Dummies. New Jersey: Wiley & Sons, 2006.

U.S. Army Judge Advocate General's Legal Center and School. 2015 Commander's Legal Handbook. Misc Pub 27-8. March 2015. Internet article, Feb 6 2017. https://www.jagcnet.army.mil/Sites/jagc.nsf/0/EE26CE7A9678A67A85257E1300563559/$File/Commanders%20Legal%20HB%202015%20C1.pdf

U.S. Department of Commerce, Census Bureau. "2010 Census Shows Second Highest Homeownership Rate on Record Despite Largest Decrease since 1940." News Release, Oct 6, 2011. Internet article, Feb 23, 2017. https://www.census.gov/newsroom/releases/archives/2010_census/cb11-cn188.html

--. "Current Population Reports: Income and Poverty in the United States: 2015." September 2016. Internet article, Feb 16, 2017. http://www.census.gov/content/dam/Census/library/publications/2016/demo/p60-256.pdf

U.S. Department of the Treasury. "Treasury Securities & Programs." Internet article, Feb 16, 2017. https://www.treasurydirect.gov/indiv/products/products.htm

U.S. Department of Veterans Affairs. "Servicemembers Group Life Insurance (SGLI)." Internet article, Jan 23, 2017. http://www.benefits.va.gov/insurance/sgli.asp

U.S. Securities and Exchange Commission. Amazon.com, Inc. (CIK: 0001018724) Form 8-K, Exhibit 99.1. Jul 24, 2007. Internet article, Feb 22, 2017. https://www.sec.gov/Archives/edgar/data/1018724/000119312507160753/dex991.htm

U.S. Small Business Administration. "Employers with 50 or More Employees." Internet article, Jan 17, 2017. https://www.sba.gov/managing-business/small-business-health-care/employers-50-or-more-employees

U.S. Social Security Administration. "2007 Report of the Board of Trustees." May 1, 2007. Internet article, Jan 17, 2017. https://www.ssa.gov/OACT/TR/TR07/tr07.pdf

--. "2016 Report of the Board of Trustees." Jun 22, 2016. Internet article, Jan 17, 2017. https://www.ssa.gov/OACT/TR/2016/tr2016.pdf

--. "Contribution and Benefit Bases, 1937-2017." Internet article, Jan 17, 2017. https://www.ssa.gov/oact/COLA/cbb.html#Series

--. "Social Security History." Internet article, Jan 17, 2017. https://www.ssa.gov/history/index.html

Warner, John T. and Saul Pleeter. "The Personal Discount Rate: Evidence from Military Downsizing Programs." The American Economic Review. Vol. 91, No. 1, Mar 2001.

White, Gregory. "Surprise! Here's the Real Long-Term Return on Owning a Home: 0%." Business Insider. May 9, 2011. Internet article, Feb 22, 2017. http://www.businessinsider.com/actually-you-dont-even-make-money-over-the-long-term-with-a-house-2011-5

10 Rules of Thumb

1. Pay yourself first... at least 10%; start early
2. Develop a budget
3. Keep debt under control (28% housing, 36% total)
4. Understand the difference between "good" and "bad" debt
5. Insure against catastrophic loss
6. Maintain an emergency expense fund (1-2 months' pay)
7. Diversify your portfolio
8. Don't ignore opportunity cost
9. Negotiation is good; competition is great
10. Don't count on Social Security

69253513R00100

Made in the USA
Lexington, KY
27 October 2017